Kids at Work

Kids at Work

The Value of Employer-Sponsored On-Site Child Care Centers

Rachel Connelly
Deborah S. DeGraff
Rachel A. Willis

2004

W.E. Upjohn Institute for Employment Research
Kalamazoo, Michigan

Library of Congress Cataloging-in-Publication Data

Connelly, Rachel.
  Kids at work : the value of employer-sponsored on-site child care centers / Rachel Connelly, Deborah S. DeGraff and Rachel A. Willis.
    p. cm.
  Includes bibliographical references and index.
  ISBN 0-88099-304-9 (pbk.: alk. paper)—ISBN 0-88099-305-7 (hardcover : alk. paper)
  1. Employer-supported day care—United States. I. DeGraff, Deborah S. II.
  Willis, Rachel A. III. Title.
  HF5549.5.D39C66 2004
  331.25'5—dc22
                                    2004001664

W.E. Upjohn Institute for Employment Research
300 S. Westnedge Avenue
Kalamazoo, Michigan 49007–4686

The facts presented in this study and the observations and viewpoints expressed are the sole responsibility of the authors. They do not necessarily represent positions of the W.E. Upjohn Institute for Employment Research.

Cover design by Alcorn Publication Design.
Index prepared by Diane Worden.
Printed in the United States of America.
Printed on recycled paper.

Contents

Tables

Acknowledgments

This study was supported by a grant from the W.E. Upjohn Institute for Employment Research. We also received assistance from the Bowdoin College Faculty Research Fund, Bowdoin's Department of Economics, and the University of North Carolina Center for Urban and Regional Studies and Department of Economics. We would like to thank Laurie Charest, Anne Clifford, William Darity, Rick Freeman, Kevin Hollenbeck, Jean Kimmel, Donna LeFebvre, Brett O'Hara, Susan Dana Russell, and Joel Schwartz for their constructive thoughts on the survey design and/or monograph. We are grateful to the anonymous reviewers for their helpful comments. Excellent research assistance was provided by Teresa Beckham, Vijay Bhagavan, Jen Blake, Stephanie Broughton, Jennifer Chase, Timothy Diette, Zhe Fan, Valerie Grassetti, Courtney Griffiths, Dawnelle Hyland, Neal McCall, Shuli Ren, Ian Williamson, and Jeff Winger. We would also like to acknowledge the publication of parts of this research in *Population Research and Policy Review* (with kind permission of Kluwer Academic Publishers) and *Industrial Relations: A Journal of Economy and Society* as referenced within. Many thanks are especially due to the employees and management of the three firms that donated their time and expertise to our data collection process.

I am not a feminist per se nor a bleeding heart liberal, though many people think I am. I am an opportunist, a pragmatist to the nth degree. There is no benefit in this company that we don't feel doesn't have a bottom line advantage or payback.

    —Company owner whose family-owned firm operates an on-site child care center for 85 employee children and grandchildren, including his own grandchild.

1

Introduction

Policy Issues and Research Questions

The last 25 years have witnessed a decline in the growth rate of the U.S. population. There have also been economic and social forces, such as welfare reform, an expansion of the Earned Income Tax Credit, and the continuing stagnation of wages of men with less than a college education, which have encouraged women to enter the labor market in ever-increasing numbers. As a result, much of the growth in the U.S. labor market has come from women and, in recent years, from a dramatic increase in the labor force participation of mothers with young children. The increased participation of this segment is also expected to be a substantial component of growth in the labor force for the next two decades. This trend has created a rising demand for child care and a greater level of work/family conflict for U.S. families with young children. All indications are that these effects of increasing women's labor force participation will continue in the near future.

Firms in the 1990s faced an inherently tighter labor market than they had in the past because of changing demographics in the United States and due to the strong economy. To satisfy their staffing needs, employers strove to entice those not in the labor force to enter. Among the groups consciously targeted have been the elderly and women with young children. In terms of the latter group, one strategy used by a small but growing number of firms is to provide employer-sponsored child care (ESCC) as part of a menu of employee benefits. In 1978, the

U.S. Department of Labor identified 105 ESCCs among U.S. companies. Since then, this number has increased dramatically. A 1998 survey found approximately 8,000 firms with on-site centers (McIntyre 2000).

These trends, which are presented in more detail in Chapter 2, raise important questions about the benefits of on-site child care. Why do some firms choose to offer ESCC while most do not? What is the value to the firm of offering ESCC? What is the value to employees of working for a firm with on-site child care? While we cannot answer all of these questions fully in this study, we take important steps in that direction. Chapter 3 explores economic theory with an eye to understanding why some firms choose to offer employer-sponsored on-site child care while others do not. The theoretical analysis is a general one that is widely applicable in the U.S. economy. Our empirical work, however, is limited to a case study approach in which we analyze two firms with on-site child care centers and one that does not have an on-site center, all in the same industry. The analysis provides some evidence as to why these companies have made the choices that they have about benefits, but we cannot generalize more widely from three firms the set of characteristics that lead some firms to offer ESCC while others do not. Similarly, while we explore the issue of the value to the firm of offering ESCC, the challenge of measuring the full benefits of on-site child care for employers is great, given the complex interaction between working conditions, productivity, compensation, and the makeup of one's labor force. Employers offering child care benefits often report positive impacts of child care programs on workers' performance, as well as reductions in turnover, absenteeism, and recruitment costs. Indeed, there has been substantial media coverage of employer and employee perceptions about these potential benefits of some of the higher-visibility programs. We review the literature on such cost savings in Chapter 3 and provide some anecdotal evidence from the firms we studied that points to benefits in these areas. However, given the information available at our study sites, we are not able to systematically analyze potential effects on productivity, turnover, or recruitment that may lead to cost savings for firms offering ESCC.

The primary contribution of this study is to analyze the value of employer-sponsored on-site child care to the employee. This is not often mentioned in firms' public rhetoric, but we expect that it is a substantial part of the cost savings of ESCC: the value to the employee of the benefit should translate directly into wage savings on the part of firms (Woodbury 1990). Chapter 3 explores the theoretical model that points to the importance of employee valuation in assessing the benefit of ESCC to the firm. Chapter 5 provides an indirect measure of employee valuation by analyzing who is using (or not using) the on-site center. If parents choose on-site center care when it is available over other options, consumer choice theory tells us that they must be better off with the on-site center. Which employees are more likely to select the on-site option? This information is important to human resource managers considering an on-site center and to policymakers evaluating possible approaches to helping parents with child care expenses. The next section of this chapter outlines the basic research questions of this indirect approach and previews our findings from Chapter 5.

We also offer a second approach to estimating employee valuation of ESCC, which is detailed in Chapter 7. This method uses a contingent valuation technique for eliciting the worth of the benefit directly from employees. Again, human resource officers and policymakers should be interested in the answer to the question, "What value does the average employee or recent hire place on the benefit of having an on-site center?" Both approaches expand our understanding of the benefit of employer-sponsored on-site child care to the employee and, therefore, to the employer as part of a compensation package. Both methods of analysis lead to the conclusion that employees derive substantial benefits from on-site centers, beyond what they would receive from a community-based child care center, and that the benefits from ESCC accrue to employees beyond the users of the on-site center. Given the difficulty firms have in assessing the value of ESCC, we believe our strategy makes an important contribution in providing an example that any medium-sized or large firm could follow to assess the potential value of ESCC to its employees.

The valuation of ESCC is also important from a public policy perspective. Child care has become a topic of intense public debate in the United States. In 1976, Congress enacted the Child and Dependent Care Tax Credit, and since then there has been a dramatic increase in federal spending on child care.[1] However, the Dependent Care Credit is only one of a wide variety of government programs subsidizing child care expenditure.[2] Welfare reform has also increased the pressure on states to coax low-income mothers into the labor market. In recent years, a number of proposals before Congress have involved tax breaks for companies offering ESCC.[3] This raises the question of why the government would need to encourage employers to do something that is in the firm's interest. If firms were better able to measure the benefits of ESCC, perhaps the tax incentive would not be necessary. On the other hand, if the positive externalities of a child receiving quality care and the reduction of work/family conflict are large enough, government incentives in this area might be justified, whatever the value to firms.[4] Regardless of one's perspective on this issue, a better measure of the value of ESCC to employees would inform decisions about optimal levels of provision and of tax incentives.

AN INDIRECT APPROACH TO VALUING EMPLOYER-SPONSORED ON-SITE CHILD CARE: PARENTAL CHOICE WHEN AN ON-SITE CENTER IS AVAILABLE

> *Hard to find good day care that you can trust.*
> —A 48-year-old female production worker explaining why she values her employer's on-site center.

> *Convenient for people who use it.*
> —A 22-year-old female production worker with no children yet, but who plans to use the company on-site center when she does have children.

While there is extensive literature that analyzes women's participation in the labor force and the type of child care selected by parents in the United States,[5] very little is known about parental choice of on-site center care. This is not surprising because most studies make use of nationally representative samples of households and the incidence of on-site center use, while increasing, is still so small as to be practically invisible, even in relatively large samples. However, ESCC is too important to ignore simply because it cannot be studied with conventional data sets. Instead, we have elected to use a case study approach, analyzing the child care arrangements of employees at three firms in the same local labor market and in the same industry.

Firms that offer on-site child care seem to be of two types. One does so as part of a corporate culture of "caring," a culture that is reflected by many aspects of the firm's benefits package and working conditions. The other offers child care as a response to a particular target employee population and/or as a response to a very tight labor market. We specifically looked for the latter type, without a full menu of family-friendly benefits because, while they have received less attention than some high-profile family-friendly firms, we feel that they hold more insights into "typical" firm behavior. Also, for companies that do not offer a wide array of family-friendly benefits, the effect of on-site child care is less intertwined with the impacts of other benefits.

Employees at two of the three firms we study have access to on-site child care, while employees at the third firm do not, allowing us to make comparisons of child care choice across these two scenarios. In addition, we collected from the employees of these three firms more detailed information than is often available about alternative sources of child care in the respondent's area, particularly the availability of relatives as potential care givers. This provides an opportunity to evaluate how the employee's individual menu of child care options affects his or her child care choice, a dimension of analysis that is often missing. Furthermore, household-level surveys usually are not extensive enough to gather information about the multiple strategies that parents often have in place to guard against the breakdown of child care arrangements and other unanticipated circumstances that create conflict between employment and caring for one's young children. The data we collected also address this gap in the literature on the determinants of child care choice.

Our findings on the use of on-site centers are quite clear. The presence of the on-site center option makes a substantial difference in the child care choices made by families with young children. A much higher percentage of parents employed at the two firms with on-site child care enrolled their children in a day care center in comparison to the employees of the firm without an on-site center. Thus, the presence of the on-site center did not simply divert attendance from community-based centers, but rather moved children out of home day care and relative care into center-based care. Also important is our finding that parents of infants are likely to use the on-site center, as are those with older children. This suggests that at least some of the national differential between modes of care for infants and preschoolers comes from a lack of slots for infants at child care centers rather than from parental preference, or that parents may value ESCC differently than other center care for infants. Although those with relatives available for providing child care are less likely to use the on-site center, there are still a number of families that reported using the center despite the availability of relatives.

Users of the on-site center are also less likely to have secondary child care arrangements, suggesting less concern about breakdown in the primary arrangement. When secondary arrangements are used, they are almost always unpaid and with relatives. Workers at the firm without an on-site center are more likely to be juggling two regular child care arrangements, which might be expected to add to the stress of the work/family balancing act.

For the two firms with on-site centers, employee job tenure is found to be positively related to on-site center use. This relationship between job tenure and center use may be evidence of a lower turnover rate for center users, but it also could be the result of the allocation of a limited number of slots on a first-come, first-served basis. Education is also found to be positively related to the use of the on-site center, which substantiates company officials' claims that having the center has been especially important for recruiting and retaining young managers, especially young women managers.

It is important to note that the cost of the on-site centers to parents, while somewhat lower than the average cost of other center-based care in the area, was about equal to the average cost for all paid child care in the area at the time of our survey. Thus, enrolling one's child in the on-site center did not represent a significant saving for most parents and may have resulted in a substantial increase in expenses for those with no-cost relative care available. This suggests that quality, reliability, and convenience are important factors in the decision making of working parents; parents get extra value from the employer-sponsored and on-site aspects of ESCC. The added value of these characteristics seems to be enough for many more employees to use the on-site center than would ordinarily use center-based care. This extra value is a part of the benefit of ESCC to the employee and, thus, to the employer.

A DIRECT APPROACH TO EMPLOYEE VALUATION OF EMPLOYER-SPONSORED ON-SITE CHILD CARE

Benefit to society.
     —Non-user of center who voted yes.

I took care of my kids.
     —Non-user who voted no.

Convenience of location, I trust people here, inexpensive.
     —User of center who voted yes.

Not fair—Don't think everyone should have to pay for it.
     —User who voted no.

Turning to the direct estimation of the benefit of ESCC to employees, we apply a contingent valuation strategy. Chapter 6 discusses some of the vast body of literature on using contingent valuation for nonmonetized commodities in the environmental and natural resources field and discusses its application to the case of employer-sponsored on-site child care. The contingent valuation technique has seldom been applied to employee benefits; nonetheless, we argue that it is appropriate for determining the value that employees derive from a benefit. Like many environmental amenities, there may be a non-use or existence value to individuals of working for a company that offers an ESCC, as well as a use value to parents who have children enrolled in the center. We test this hypothesis using data collected from the three sample firms.

The findings presented in Chapter 7 indicate that price is a significant determinant of employees' votes on whether they would be willing to pay for the continued existence of the on-site center in the case of the firms that have a center, or would be willing to pay part of the cost of running a center in the case of the firm that does not have a center. We find substantial evidence of a non-use value even for employees with no young children. The results also indicate a greater valuation among recent hires than among longer-term employees, as expected. Using the statistical results, we calculate the total value that employees receive from the center, as well as the value to subgroups of employees. Any firm engaging in this exercise could then compare the cost of the benefit with the direct value to its employees, recalling that other gains such as reduced turnover, absenteeism, or recruitment costs that accrue to the firm but not directly to the employees are not included in these calculations.

RESEARCH DESIGN

Our empirical analysis is based on a case study approach involving three firms in the same labor market and in the same industry. Two of the firms offer on-site child care to employees, while the third does not. This case study approach has important advantages. Because the firms' employees live in the same area, their market child care options are identical; their menus of child care choices differ only in the availability of on-site care, and of relatives willing to provide child care, and in their access to means-tested government subsidy programs. Sampling within a relatively small geographic area also controls for other unobservables such as differences in the cost of living and regional unemployment rates. Furthermore, very simply, the concentration of sampling within firms that have on-site child care renders this type of analysis feasible when the incidence of on-site child care use is still almost imperceptible in the population as a whole.

We recognize, however, that there is also a disadvantage to using firms in the same local labor market in that employees may choose among firms based on the benefits available at each company. This might be exactly a firm's intention in offering on-site child care, but it introduces endogeneity between who works for which firm and parental choice of child care. Accounting for the endogeneity of firm choice is beyond the limits of a three-firm case study. Instead, we try to be cautious in the interpretation of results, emphasizing the unique aspects of these data while exploring the effects of an on-site center in parental decision making and deriving estimates of the value of ESCC.

An employee survey, which is discussed more fully in Chapter 4, was used to gather information about current child care arrangements for employees with young children, alternative child care options, basic socioeconomic and demographic characteristics of all sample employees and their households, and contingent valuation responses. Our survey includes 904 employees of whom 259 have a child under age six. The employees represented by our data all work for one of three light manufacturing firms in the same industry in the area of a midsized city in the Southeast of the United States. Women represent the vast majority of the production workers in this industry. Survey responses were collected through in-person interviews on company time. We spent time in each firm during working hours, interviewed workers on all shifts, and talked informally with supervisors and plant managers. We spoke extensively with the human resource officers and top administrators at each of the three firms regarding their choices about benefit spending and particularly about ESCC. Thus, with this unique case study, we are able to contribute interesting insights about several largely unexplored aspects of ESCC, most importantly, parental decisions related to the use of on-site centers versus other child care options, and the economic value to employees of ESCC.

The study proceeds as follows. Chapter 2 provides background information on trends in women's labor force participation, the use of nonparental child care, and employer sponsorship of child care in the United States. Chapter 3 develops a theoretical framework for understanding why firms might choose to offer a benefit such as ESCC, and for identifying the sources of employee benefits from employer-sponsored on-site child care. Chapter 3 also summarizes the limited research that has focused on ESCC, providing an overview that cannot be found elsewhere in the literature. The study sites and data collection, which are common to both of our analyses of ESCC, are discussed in Chapter 4. Chapter 5 presents the indirect analysis of employee benefits from ESCC, a comparison of use patterns for employees with and without an on-site child care option. Chapters 6 and 7 focus on the direct measurement of employee valuation of the benefits of ESCC. Chapter 6 contains an overview of the contingent valuation methodology and how we use it for our specific case. Chapter 7 discusses the estimated contingent valuation equations for the three firms in our study and describes the resulting willingness-to-pay estimates. Finally, Chapter 8 summarizes the history of government policy regarding child care funding, focusing particularly on ESCC and concludes with recommendations to firms that are considering offering ESCC and to government policymakers who are thinking about providing tax incentives or other interventions to encourage employer-sponsored on-site child care.

Notes

1. In 1999, the cost of the Child and Dependent Care Credit was estimated to be $2.8 billion (Blau 2000).
2. See Blau (2000) for a history of major government programs that subsidize child care.
3. There is currently no federal tax incentive for companies offering ESCC, but several states give tax credits to employers for costs related to ESCC.
4. See Vandell and Wolfe (2000) for a full discussion of potential externalities of child care quality.
5. See, for example, Blau and Robins (1988), Blau and Hagy (1998), Brayfield and Hofferth (1995), Connelly and Kimmel (2003), Duncan and Hill (1977), Folk and Beller (1993), Han (1999), Hofferth and Wissoker (1992), Johansen, Leibowitz, and Waite (1996), Kimmel (1995, 1998), Lehrer (1983, 1989), Leibowitz, Waite, and Witsberger (1988), Mason and Kuhlthau (1989), and Ribar (1992, 1995).

2

The Labor Market and Child Care Context in the United States

TRENDS IN WOMEN'S LABOR FORCE PARTICIPATION

The tremendous increase in women's labor force participation in the second half of the twentieth century has truly transformed the American labor market. In 1962, 36.6 percent of women were employed. By 2001, this percentage had increased to 59.7 (U.S. Census Bureau 2002a, Table 561). Traditionally, married women's employment had been well below the employment rates of never-married and divorced women. The rates for all three groups increased over this period, with the married women's rate of labor force participation growing the fastest. Today, divorced and never-married women still have a higher level of labor force participation than currently married women. Also, in recent years, a larger percentage of women fall into those categories with higher rates of participation, given the older age of first marriage and greater rates of divorce that women experience today as compared to the past. The rise in women's labor force participation from all sources of change, coupled with a slight decline in men's labor force participation, especially among very young and older males, has caused the proportion of the labor force that is female to increase from 33.3 percent in 1960 to 46.5 percent in 1999 (U.S. Census Bureau 1995, Table 631; 2000, Table 647).

While early in this "revolution" of women's employment, older women with grown children constituted the largest group among those entering the labor market, during the 1980s and 1990s, one of the fastest growing segments of the labor force was women with young children. The labor force participation rate of married women with children under age six increased from 30.3 percent in 1970 to 45.1 percent in 1980, to 58.9 percent in 1990, and to 63.5 percent in 1995 (U.S. Census Bureau 2002a, Table 570). Employment rates for women with even younger children have also increased. For example, the labor force participation rate of married women with children under age three rose from 21.2 percent in 1966 to 32.7 percent in 1975, to 50.5 percent in 1985, to 59.7 percent in 1994, and remained at 59.4 percent in 2001 (Blau, Ferber, and Winkler 1998, p. 95; U.S. Census Bureau 2002a, Table 571). As the employment of women with young children continues to grow, child care that can facilitate employment has also gained in importance to American families and employers.

In addition to entering the labor force in large numbers, women have increased the number of hours they work in the labor market. For example, in 1969, 27.5 percent of all women aged 25 to 54 worked full-time; by 1997, this percentage had increased to 50.2 (U.S. Department of Labor 1999a). Given that unemployment was very low for most of the 1990s, firms seeking to expand or even maintain their workforce simply could not ignore women workers or even women workers with young children.

The increase in the number of women workers and in the hours they are employed has led to a variety of changes in the ways families try to meet the custodial and developmental needs of young children. While married fathers spend more time with their children than in earlier decades and provide a substantial proportion of child care when the mother works part-time, children of full-time women workers are less likely to be cared for by their fathers while their mothers are at work (Bianchi 2000). The percentage of children's households with two parents, one of whom is not in the labor force, has steadily decreased over time and is now clearly a minority. For example, in 1999, 46.5 percent of families with children under the age of 18 had two earners, 27.5 percent were single-parent households (almost 20 percent of these were father-only households), and only 26 percent of families with children had two parents in residence with only one (or no, for a small percentage) employed parent (U.S. Census Bureau 2000, Table 655). Furthermore, for children under the age of 18 in two-parent households, the ratio of father's time to mother's time spent with children has increased from 0.51 to 0.65 between 1965 and 1998 (Bianchi 2000).[1] Even where the father is not providing child care, he may be involved in transporting the child to day care or doing other household tasks that in the past were handled by a stay-at-home mother. Consequently, men with young children as well as women with young children may value efforts by employers to help ease work/family tension.

TRENDS IN THE USE OF NONPARENTAL CHILD CARE

By the end of the 1990s, slightly fewer than one-fourth of pre-school children aged three to five in the United States were regularly cared for only by parents. The incidence of sole parental care for this group declined by almost 8 percentage points from 1991 to 1999. In conjunction with this trend, the regular use of some type of day care center or preschool among this group increased from about 53 to almost 60 percent during the same time period (U.S. Census Bureau 2001, Table 557). These statistics reflect an overall increase in the demand for nonparental child care, regardless of the mother's employment status. Evolving work patterns can be expected to result in even greater changes in the pattern of child care used by employed mothers with young children.

Table 2.1 shows the distribution of child care arrangements for pre-school age children with employed mothers, as obtained from national data for selected years from 1977 to 1999 (U.S. Census Bureau 1998; Smith 2002, Table 3; U.S. Census Bureau 2003). The data used in Table 2.1, with the exception of 1977, come from the Survey of Income and Program Participation (SIPP), a nationally representative survey conducted on a regular basis by the U.S. Census Bureau. Looking at Table 2.1, we see that until 1994 the combined percentage of children being cared for by a relative or by a nonrelative in a home-based day care arrangement decreased over time, while the percentage being cared for in a child care center or in a nursery school increased. This may reflect the changing needs of employed mothers in that those working full-time may prefer the regularized care of a center compared to a relative, or may have fewer relatives available for care as families become more geographically dispersed and more relatives may be in the labor force themselves. In addition, it may also reflect an increased demand for early childhood education. We know that a substantial number of preschoolers are enrolled in early childhood education programs even if there is a parent at home (Hotz and Kilburn 1992).

Data for 1995 and 1997 are difficult to compare with earlier years due to several changes in the questionnaire and in the way the data were collected. Taken at face value, we see that some of the earlier trends in child care arrangements have been reduced or at least damp-

Table 2.1 Primary Child Care Arrangements Used for Preschoolers by Families with Employed Mothers in the United States, Selected Years, 1977 to 1999

Type of arrangement	Fall[a] 1977	Fall 1985	Fall 1986	Fall 1987	Fall 1988	Fall 1990	Fall 1991	Fall 1993	Fall 1994	Fall 1995[b]	Spring 1997[c]	Spring 1999
Number of children (000s)	4,370	8,168	8,849	9,124	9,483	9,629	9,854	9,937	10,288	10,047	10,116	10,587
% care:												
By father	14.4	15.7	14.5	15.3	15.1	16.5	20.0	15.9	18.5	16.6	19.0	19.3
By grandparent		15.9	15.4	13.8	13.9	14.3	15.8	17.0	16.3	15.9	18.4	21.7
By other relative	30.9[d]	8.2	9.9	7.9	7.2	8.8	7.7	9.0	9.0	5.5	7.4	8.4
By nonrelative	29.4	28.2	29.5	28.5	28.9	25.1	23.3	21.6	20.5	28.4	22.1	21.1
Organized child care facilities and school-based activity	13.0	23.1	22.4	24.4	26.0	27.5	23.1	29.9	29.6	25.1	21.7	25.9
Child cares for self and other arrangements[e]	1.0	0.8	0.8	1.3	1.4	1.3	1.6	1.1	0.9	2.9	8.1	4.8
Mother cares for child at work[f]	11.4	8.1	7.4	8.9	7.6	6.4	8.7	6.2	5.5	5.4	3.3	3.2

[a] Data only for the two youngest children under 5 years of age.
[b] Survey design changes make comparison with previous years difficult. The number of categories was expanded, including the option of saying "no regular arrangement."
[c] Paper questionnaires of the past were replaced by computer-based surveying. Also time of year of survey changed and may contribute to differences in the arrangement distribution. Column percentages may sum to more than 100 because of a small percentage of children with two primary care arrangements listed.
[d] Data for 1977 include grandparents.
[e] Includes children in kindergarten/grade school and "no regular arrangement" for 1995 and 1997.
[f] Includes mothers working for pay at home or away from home.
SOURCE: U.S. Census Bureau (1998b); Smith (2002); U.S. Census Bureau (2003).

ened, with relative care rebounding and center-based care losing 8 percentage points. Lest we attribute all of this to changes in the survey, data from the National Survey of American Families show a similar decline in center care and an increase in relative care. Sonenstein et al. (2002) find that between 1997 and 1999, the child care arrangements of children of employed parents shifted away from center-based care, with the proportion cared for in centers declining from 32 percent to 28 percent of children four years old and younger. Care by relatives increased from 23 to 27 percent during the same two-year period. These changes are confined to children from two-parent families, regardless of income. The pattern of child care arrangements for single-parent families remained unchanged over the period, with close to 40 percent of these families using center care (Sonenstein et al. 2002). It is unclear whether changes in government support or in availability help to explain the reduction in the proportion of young children using center-based care. It may reflect heterogeneity among the recent new entrants into the labor market. As a result of the tight labor market, which attracts individuals who otherwise would not be employed, it is possible that many new entrants into the labor market are piecing together relative care instead of using center care, either because they are more committed to relative care, because they do not plan to stay in the labor market very long, or because their incomes are lower on average.

As the statistics from Sonenstein et al. (2002) indicate, marital status is one dimension across which child care usage clearly differs. Single mothers rely more on center care and relative care and are much less likely to use home-based care by nonrelatives. Part of their use of centers may be because government subsidies such as those provided by Title IA funds and the Child Care and Development Fund are more often directed at center-based care. Smith (2002) shows the distribution of types of arrangements used by children under age five, comparing those for whom government assistance for child care costs is received and those for whom it is not. Forty-three percent of children whose parents receive government help with child care expenses were in center care compared to 20 percent of those whose parents do not receive government help with child care. Twenty percent of those who received government help with child care expenses were cared for by nonrelatives in the child's or the caregiver's home compared with 18 percent of those not receiving government help (Smith 2002, p. 19). Similarly, Connelly and Kimmel (2003, p. 769) find that only 71 percent of single mothers who are employed full-time and are using center-based care report paying for that care, compared to 81 percent of the married mothers employed full-time and using center-based care. On the other hand, they find that single mothers are much more likely to pay their relatives who are providing care than are married mothers. For married women, higher nonlabor income (which is largely husband's income) is correlated with a greater use of center care and a reduction in care by relatives. While some of this difference may reflect preferences, it may also indicate access to certain types of care. Center care tends to be the most expensive. In addition, relatives of high-income women are themselves more likely to be high-income earners and, thus, the opportunity cost of them watching young children is greater.

Connelly and Kimmel (2003) also find using SIPP data that child care arrangements differ by a number of other characteristics of the family, including employment status of the mother, race and ethnicity, education, and income. For example, mothers who work full-time are more likely to use center care than mothers who work part-time. In addition, characteristics of the children, particularly age and the number and ages of siblings, also affect the type of care arrangement chosen. Consistent with other studies, Connelly and Kimmel (2003) find that children under age two are less likely to be in center care than are children aged three to five. They also find that, for single mothers, preschool children with siblings who are also preschoolers are less likely to be cared for by relatives, and that, for married mothers, preschool children with siblings who are of school age (6 to 12 years old) are less likely to be cared for in centers. The presence of teenage siblings also reduces the likelihood that a preschool child is cared for in a center (Connelly and Kimmel 2003, p. 771).

CHILD CARE EXPENDITURES

Parents spend a substantial amount of money on child care. Table 2.2 shows the average price of full-time child care of various types for

Table 2.2 Weekly Full-Time Child Care Costs for Children under Five Years of Age with Employed Mothers in the United States,[a] Spring 1997

Type of arrangement	Mean weekly expenditure[b]
All children	$70.13
Care by:	
Grandparents	$40.30
Other relatives[c]	$49.18
In-home babysitters	$56.95
Family day care	$68.62
Other nonrelative	$51.38
Day care center	$86.44
Nursery/preschool	$56.19

[a] Includes only respondents paying for care.
[b] Includes only children with a regular child care arrangement.
[c] Excludes fathers and siblings.
SOURCE: Smith (2002).

children of employed mothers in the United States in 1997 for those respondents paying for care (Smith 2002). Many child care arrangements with relatives are unpaid. Only 15 percent of grandparents who provided child care were paid in 1997, and 28 percent of other relatives. In comparison, 91 percent of home-based day care provided by nonrelatives and 86 percent of day care arrangements overall were paid (Smith 2002, p. 14). For all those paying for an arrangement, parents spent, on average, about $70 per week on child care in 1997 (Smith 2002, p. 14). Day care centers appear to be the most expensive type of care, whereas child care provided by grandparents and relatives costs much less.

For the average family that is not poor, child care expenses in 1997 represented about 7 percent of family income. For a poor family, child care expenses, while lower absolutely, represented a larger proportion of income, 20 percent in 1997 (Smith 2002, p. 17). For a single mother with a minimum wage job, an average child care expenditure would represent 30.6 percent of her income (Casper 1995). With expenses this high, it is not surprising that the reservation wage of some women with young children is above their offered market wage. In other words, they are out of the labor force because it "does not pay" for them to be employed. Therefore, companies may be able to bring these women into the labor market through subsidies for work-related child care expenditures.[2] We now describe to what extent firms have done so in the form of providing employer-sponsored on-site child care.

TRENDS IN THE PROVISION OF EMPLOYER-SPONSORED CHILD CARE (ESCC)

In 1978, the U.S. Department of Labor identified 105 companies in the United States with ESCC programs. Since then, the number has increased dramatically. According to the Conference Board, the total grew to 600 in 1982, to 2,000 in 1984, to 2,500 in 1985, and to 3,500 in 1988 (Wash and Brand 1990). Ten years later, in 1998, approximately 8,000 firms provided on-site child care, and many others offered some other form of child care assistance (McIntyre 2000). Despite this substantial growth, ESCC is still only provided by a small percentage of firms. A study that surveyed 1,057 for-profit companies and not-for-profit organizations with 100 or more employees found that child care was provided by just 9 percent of the total surveyed (McIntyre 2000).

These statistics raise two questions: what caused the upturn in the number of companies offering ESCC, and simultaneously, why is the percentage of companies offering ESCC still so small? We believe that the increase in the number of companies offering ESCC is related to the trends in women's employment previously outlined. A greater percentage of the workforce is female, and many of these women have young children. The tight labor markets of the 1990s also, undoubtedly, contributed to the search for new benefits to draw women not in the labor force into employment. For example, consider the situation of Lancaster Laboratories, a firm of 150 employees in 1986, which found that it was losing skilled workers who left the company after having a baby. Its employees were mainly young and mostly women, and a survey found that many of them planned to have a child in the next five years but, also, that they planned to continue being employed if they could find child care. The company responded by opening an on-site center. The firm now reports an annual turnover rate of only 8 percent, which is half of the average for this industry (U.S. Department of Treasury 1998).

Beginning in the mid 1980s, publications aimed at human resource managers urged corporate officers to consider child care benefits as part of their new efforts to address work/family conflict (see, for example: Adolf and Rose 1985; Galinsky 1986; and Ribaric 1987). In 1994, Creed, Allen, and Whitney listed on-site day care and flexible working hours as the two biggest areas for growth in benefits plans. Furthermore, there has also been limited evidence of public support for such initiatives. For example, a 1996 Gallup Poll indicated that almost 60 percent of workers surveyed would be willing to contribute some percentage of their income to support on-site child care, with little difference in results between those with and without young children (McIntyre 2000).

The answer to why the number is still so small is, in part, that employer-sponsored on-site child care does not make sense for every firm. The value of ESCC will depend on firm size, employee demographics, and location. Some areas may have adequate supplies of community-based child care or may find themselves with plenty of job applicants. Even firms that might benefit from ESCC may not adopt it because they find it difficult to measure the benefits and, thus, they cannot evaluate whether it would be cost effective. In a survey of over 1,000 firms, each with more than 100 employees, one-third of them cited cost as the main business obstacle to implementing ESCC. Also listed were administrative hassles, competitive pressures, and a belief that the programs are not cost effective (U.S. Department of Treasury 1998). However, the majority (76 percent) of firms that reported offering ESCC believed that these programs are either cost neutral or have benefits to the firm that outweigh the costs (Families and Work Institute 1998).

There is also a reluctance to experiment with benefits because it is more costly to employee morale to eliminate an existing benefit than it is advantageous to add one. Flynn (1995) reflects this reluctance as he cautions human resource managers to move carefully on child care. He states that while such programs are popular with employees, many companies are reluctant to invest in them because there is not a clear understanding of the return they will bring. In terms of on-site centers, the primary concern is that the benefit affects only a small proportion of most workforces. Therefore, according to Flynn, an on-site child care program may be most effective for organizations with a large number of employees with dependent children. Similarly, Benson and Whatley (1994) and Sprague (1998), urge human resource managers to carefully determine which child care option best satisfies their firm's requirements. According to Benson and Whatley (1994), Sprague (1998), and McIntyre (2000), the advantages of on-site child care are its convenience, reliability, high visibility, and ability to control. The disadvantages include limited capacity and options, potential inequality, and relatively high costs. Many of the articles we surveyed suggest a need for more systematic studies of child care benefits to assess whether they have the expected effect on recruitment, retention, absenteeism, and productivity in order to better understand their value to firms and, implicitly, to employees.

Notes

1. See Presser (1988, 1989, 1995) for an analysis of couples working at different times of the day to cover their child-care needs with less or no use of nonparental child care.
2. The emphasis here is on the word *may*. Child care costs are only one of the reasons young mothers may not be in the labor market. Some will choose to stay at home even if offered free child care because of other costs of employment, the opportunity cost of home production foregone, and/or the value they receive from providing child care, either in terms of benefits to the child or directly to themselves.

3
Economic Framework for the Valuation of ESCC

Child care is not for everybody in every location. The things that make child care work for us are the low turnover rate, the high female work population, the fact that most of these jobs, the line jobs, require a great level of energy and appeal to women that are in their childbearing age. When they get beyond their childbearing age, it is hard for them to do some of the production jobs that are here. So, our work population stays currently in that group that needs child care.
—Action Industries human resource officer

In this chapter, we first develop a theoretical framework for analyzing firm behavior regarding employer-sponsored on-site child care, building on the economic theory of employee benefits. We then summarize past research on the benefits of ESCC and briefly discuss how the analysis presented here differs from previous work. The purpose is to place the analysis presented in later chapters into perspective, in terms of economic theory and of research in this field.

MODELING THE FIRM'S CHOICE OF BENEFITS AS A COST-MINIMIZING STRATEGY

Economic models of employee benefits begin with the assumption that firms seek to maximize profits by reducing costs of producing a given quantity of goods. Given this cost-minimizing perspective, a firm would choose to provide compensation in the form of benefits rather than wages if there is some financial advantage to doing so. Many types of financial advantages are possible. A given benefit may increase work incentives, thereby reducing shirking or absenteeism and/or increasing worker productivity per hour. There may be a tax or cost advantage to the firm or to the employee of benefit versus wage compensation. Finally, the benefit could reduce turnover costs or allow the firm to attract similar workers with a lower-cost compensation package. Turnover would be reduced if the benefit increases the value of the employer/employee match to the worker; examples include a pension that takes years to be fully vested or health insurance that excludes existing conditions and, thus, encourages workers to remain with their current employer once covered.

A number of studies have focused on the effectiveness of ESCC in reducing absenteeism or turnover and in increasing the level of commitment the employee feels to the firm. These articles are reviewed in the next section. There is also the tax advantage to the employer and to the employee of providing compensation in the form of a benefit instead of as money earnings. In addition to the standard tax advantage of any benefit, in some states there are special tax advantages for employers for ESCC, but these are typically small.[1] Given the lack of economies of scale in the provision of child care, it is unlikely that there are important cost advantages to firms offering child care over other providers in the child care market.[2] However, other child care providers offer a slightly different service than does an on-site center. Only the employer can provide employer-sponsored child care, and only the employer can provide child care that is located at the place of work. Workers may value these two aspects of ESCC if they are thought of as increasing the quality of the child care arrangement through the employer sponsorship, or as lowering the cost per unit of quality through the on-site location. If workers do value these aspects of ESCC, then, holding everything else constant, an employer that provides ESCC could reduce its compensation package in other ways and attract and retain similar workers. Our study of parental choice of on-site child care focuses on the employer-sponsored and on-site nature of ESCC provision.

In addition to providing the valued commodities of employer sponsorship and convenience of location, the employer that provides an ESCC benefit in a tight labor market may be able to reap substantial direct cost savings on their total compensation bill and recruitment costs. The main argument here is that the firm saves money by targeting the benefit, which is a form of additional compensation, at the group it most wants to attract into the labor market without having to offer higher wages to all of its current employees. Consider a firm with two types of workers, those with young children, YC, and those without, N. Assume that YC and N are perfect substitutes in the production function so that the level of output, $Q = f(YC + N, K)$, where K is capital equipment. In order to attract more women with young children into the labor market, the firm must raise the compensation of workers with young children, C_{YC}. Other workers are already in the labor market and thus do not require an increase in compensation, C_N. However, in an industry where workers are paid a common production wage, that is, a payment per item produced, the firm cannot simply raise wages for one group, w_{YC}, without also increasing wages for the other group, w_N. In other words, the production wage, w, is such that $w = w_N = w_{YC}$. Thus, to attract new workers into the labor market using higher money wages, the firm would have to give all workers a raise. However, if $C_{YC} = w_{YC} + B_{YC}$, where B_{YC} is the per-hour value of employee benefits, and $C_N = w_N + B_N$, the firm could increase C_{YC} without increasing C_N by choosing a benefit expenditure valued by workers with young children. It seems reasonable that under some circumstances the fixed cost to the firm of the benefit will be less than the cost of increasing the production wage for all employees.

Even in industries where wages are not production-based, a firm may find it difficult to raise one group of workers' wages without raising those of other workers. The firm may be concerned with antidiscrimination laws or may be worried about loss of productivity of some workers if they learn about the relative differences in their wages. Research in this area often talks about the ripple effect that an increase in the minimum wage can have on nonminimum wage workers. Similarly, one could argue that firms trying to attract women with young children into the labor market with higher money wage offers may be concerned about bidding up their entire wage distribution.

If a potential worker's employment decision is affected by the cost of child care, then employers should be able to entice some individuals into the labor market by offering an ESCC. What evidence do we have that the compensation level affects the decision of women with young children to enter the labor market? Standard economic theory suggests that the high costs of child care decrease the effective hourly return to employment, thus reducing the probability that a woman with young children participates in the labor market. Empirically, one of the most stable results from studies of the determinants of women's labor force participation in the United States has been the negative effect of young children on participation. This relationship continues to be significant for the presence of very young children despite the substantial increase in the labor force participation of women with young children. In addition, a more recent set of empirical studies has focused on the effect of child care costs on women's labor market behavior and has consistently found a significant negative effect of the cost of child care on a woman's decision to participate in the labor force.[3]

Our study of the contingent valuation of the ESCC benefit focuses on the money savings to the firm for providing ESCC instead of raising the money wage. The lower total wage bill is potentially one of the most important benefits that a firm would expect to gain through an ESCC, but it is not the benefit that firms publicize, nor one that has been studied. Firms tend to talk about happier employees and better cared-for children, with the inevitable picture of the company president surrounded by a group of darling toddlers. The research we discuss has tended to focus on reduced turnover and absenteeism, and on higher levels of organizational commitment. To calculate the value to firms of the savings in the wage bill, we must know what increase in wages the firm would have had to offer to attract another worker, and by how much other wages would have been bid up as a result of this increase. To estimate the former, one must know the value the new hire receives from the child care benefit. Although it is tempting, it is incorrect to simply use the per-employee cost of the employer subsidy as a proxy for the value to the employee (Samulari and Manser 1989). Some employees may value the ESCC more than the subsidy if, for example, the firm's endorsement of the child care center gives them a greater sense of trust about their child's well-being or if the on-site location adds significantly to the value of the child care. Other employees may value it less than the subsidy if, for example, they could have used a relative or a friend to provide lower cost child care than the full cost of the ESCC, or if they do not have young children.

The full savings to the total wage bill can be calculated by multiplying the value of the benefit to the new hire, B_{YC}, by either the total number of employee hours, $YC + N$, if we assume an across-the-board pay increase would have been needed, or the total number of entry-level employee hours, if we assume that only entry-level wages would have had to increase to accomplish the goal of hiring new employees.[4] Under the former assumption, which we argue is more appropriate in this industry and labor market, the idea is that, were it not for the

ESCC, w_{YC} would have to be raised to attract the new hire, but then all employees would receive the higher w_{YC} because $w_{YC} = w_N$; that is, the firm cannot distinguish between the employees in a way that is feasible or perhaps legal. The full value to the employer of offering ESCC then would be the sum of the savings in direct compensation and the cost savings accruing to the firm from other positive effects of the benefit, such as increased worker productivity through improved worker morale, reduced absenteeism, and lower turnover rates, and savings in direct recruitment costs. Thus, while the value that the new hire places on the ESCC is not the only source of cost savings for the firm from offering an ESCC, it is at least theoretically an important part of the story. We use the results of the contingent valuation multivariate analysis to estimate the value of the ESCC to individuals who have been employed by the firm for less than two years and use this amount to calculate the firm's total savings in wage compensation.

While the firm's main concern may be new hires, from the workers' perspective, both new and long-term employees have the potential to gain from the offering of an additional benefit. Firms (and governments) may also be interested in this information as indicative of the level of externalities, both positive and negative, that would be generated by the benefit. Furthermore, employee valuation of the benefit may give the firm some indication of the potential for accruing other cost savings, as previously described, such as the reduction in absenteeism and lower turnover rates. One might conjecture that employees who value a benefit highly will be less likely to leave the firm for employment elsewhere. Thus, we argue that there is interest in calculating the value of ESCC to all employees, not just to newly hired employees. The methodology for calculating that value is discussed in Chapter 6, and the results are presented in Chapter 7.

REVIEW OF PREVIOUS RESEARCH ON THE BENEFITS OF ESCC

In previous research on employer-sponsored on-site child care, the primary benefit ascribed from this to the firm is increased productivity of workers whose concerns about work/family conflict are eased. This improvement, it is argued, leads to savings on the part of the company sponsoring the child care, savings that may be greater than the cost of the program. In addition, the firm may save money in the area of recruitment and training if ESCC helps the firm retain productive workers.

Increased productivity is difficult to measure in the service sector, but even in manufacturing, highly decentralized industrial processes with large components of support services make it difficult to observe marginal productivity directly. Instead, most studies of the effects of employee benefits have focused on proxies for productivity, such as turnover, absenteeism, performance levels, and tardiness. In addition, some attempts have been made to include measurement of employee attitudes, such as job motivation or satisfaction (Kossek and Nichol 1992; Rothausen et al. 1998; Rubin et al. 1989).

Past research can be divided into two types of analyses: employer-based and employee-based. The former seeks to test theories of benefits package selection by employers and looks at the choice to offer family-responsive benefits as a function of observable characteristics of the firm. The latter tries to measure employee response to the provision of family-friendly benefits. Both types of studies suffer from standard problems of statistical analysis: low response rates and the potential biasing effects of unobservable variables and endogeneity. In addition, sample sizes may be limited by the size of the firm itself.

Employer-Based Research

Several researchers have tried to model what type of firm is most likely to offer a child care benefit as part of its benefits package. Proponents of the rational choice model argue that firms most likely to experience cost savings as a result of providing the benefit are the most likely to offer it. Glass and Fujimoto (1995) test the rational choice model against two alternative theories that can be characterized as bureaucratic control and paternalism. The bureaucratic control theory argues that employers offer family-responsive policies as a way to maintain bureaucratic control of the employees. The theory of paternalism suggests that family responsiveness is embedded in the individual values and norms of the employer. Glass and Fujimoto attempt to test among these three explanations for firms choosing ESCC and others that have not. This is a difficult task owing to a lack of observable characteristics of the firm that can differentiate among the three theories. Our reading of their empirical evidence is that rational choice is at least still in the running.

One of the variables that significantly affects the probability that a firm offers ESCC in Glass and Fujimoto's study is whether the employees are unionized. The researchers find that unionized firms are less likely to provide ESCC and argue that because of the majority rules aspect of union operations, such organizations are less likely to support a benefit that directly affects only some of the employees. Glass and Fujimoto also find that firm size is positively related to child care benefits while, surprisingly, female concentration of the workforce has no effect on child care benefits. In a similar study, Seyler, Monroe and Garand (1995) find a significant positive effect of female concentration on the probability of a firm offering family benefits. In this study, in which human resource officers at 290 firms were surveyed, the size of the company and the percentage of female employees are consistently positively related to the offering of family benefits. Other variables—the average age of employees, the firm's level of investment in recruiting and training, and the educational level required for employees—are not significant predictors.

The *Business Work-Life Study* (Families and Work Institute 1998) considered the question of what companies are most likely to provide work-life programs, more broadly defined. Industry, company size, and the proportion of the top executive positions filled by women and minorities were found to be important predictors of work-life programs. Six times as many companies with a majority of women in top executive positions provide on- or near-site child care as those with no women in top management (Families and Work Institute 1998, p. XII). The direction of causality is not clear because the availability of on-site care may encourage women with children to take (and keep) jobs at the company, or the presence of women in top positions may mean that management is more aware of child care concerns.

Finally, Auerbach (1990) surveyed 90 employers in 1986 in a local labor market in order to determine which firms are most likely to provide child care benefits. Firms with a higher concentration of women employees, that are non-unionized, that offer other creative benefits, and that have relatively progressive employment policies and philosophies are more likely to offer child care benefits. Five reasons were given by employers for sponsoring child care: 1) recruitment and retention of personnel; 2) reduction of absenteeism and turnover; 3) sense of social responsibility; 4) public relations; and 5) demand from current employees. The first element, recruitment and retention, is the primary reason stated. Barriers to providing child care include lack of perceived demand, costs, equity concerns, liability, licensing, and space (Auerbach 1990).

Employee-Based Research

Turning to employee response to family benefits, there have been only a few studies that have tried to measure the effect of ESCC programs on proxies of productivity, e.g., labor force participation, absenteeism, turnover, and commitment to employer. Several others have looked at family-friendly benefits more generally. Of the studies that have focused on ESCC, most have shown its beneficial effects on turnover, recruitment, satisfaction, and morale (Auerbach 1990; Friedman 1989; Goff, Mount, and Jamison 1990; Marquart 1988; Milkovich and Gomez 1976; Rothausen et al. 1998; Roth and Preston 1989; Shellenbarger 1992; Youngblood and Chambers-Cook 1974). For example, Roth and Preston (1989) found a decrease in turnover of 3 to 8 percent after the adoption of an on-site child care center. They also found greater job satisfaction and job commitment after the adoption of on-site child care. Rothausen et al. (1998) measured employee attitudes both toward the on-site center specifically, and more generally toward the firm and the working environment. They found that the use of the center is not related to general work attitudes, although it was related to workers' perceptions of a recruiting and retention effect of offering on-site child care and to their satisfaction with the amount of support the company provides for day care programs. Lehrer, Santero, and Mohan-Neill (1991) looked at annual hours worked and attachment to employer for registered nurses. They found that employer-sponsored child care significantly increased both measures of labor supply.

The findings on the effect of ESCC on productivity, absenteeism, and performance are more mixed. For example, Krug, Palmour, and Ballassai (1972) find no statistically significant impact of ESCC participation on tardiness and absenteeism. In contrast, Milkovich and

Gomez (1976) find a statistically significant difference in the absentee-ism and turnover rates for 30 participants in ESCC compared to that of a group of 30 employees with children not participating in the program. Miller (1984) argues that both of these early studies suffer from serious statistical and research design flaws. Goff, Mount, and Jamison (1990) surveyed 253 employees with children under age six of a large Mid-western electronics firm.[5] Comparing users of the on-site center to non-users, they find no significant differences in the level of work/family conflict, pre-treatment absenteeism, and post-treatment absenteeism. On the other hand, they find more generally that the level of work/fam-ily conflict experienced by employed parents is significantly related to absenteeism. The level of work/family conflict is linked to supportive supervision and satisfaction with one's own child care arrangement. If the level of satisfaction with the on-site child care center is greater than the average level of satisfaction with child care arrangements in gen-eral, then on-site centers would reduce absenteeism. Kossek and Nichol (1992) used a matched supervisor/employee data set with 155 employee respondents. Like Milkovich and Gomez (1976), they find the use of on-site child care to be unrelated to performance, but, unlike Milkovich and Gomez, they also find no direct effect on absenteeism. In addition, they find a "frustration" effect among those employees whose children are on the waiting list for the center. These wait-listed employees were less likely to perceive the child care benefit as fair and had lower ratings of the attractiveness of the benefit to the firm.

Looking at studies of family-friendly benefits more generally, Greenberger et al. (1989) surveyed 321 employed parents of preschool children. Their goal was to assess the contribution of informal social workplace support and formal family-responsive benefits on job-related attitudes and personal well-being of employed parents. They find that women make significantly greater use of family-responsive benefits than do men. In addition, greater formal workplace support increases the level of organizational commitment among both married and single women, and increases job satisfaction and well-being among married women. Furthermore, they conclude that informal social workplace support and formal benefits have an additive effect on well-being and are not redundant. Using the same data, Goldberg et al. (1989) report on the responses to questions about how much of which employer benefit and policy would entice workers to leave their present employer for another who offered the particular benefit or policy. They find that working parents with young children look to the workplace for assistance with child care. Thirty to 40 percent of men and women indicate that they would leave their jobs to change to another one that offered child care near the job site.

Grover and Crooker (1995) used data from the General Social Survey, 1991, to examine the impact of family-responsive policies on employees' level of work commitment, as measured by an eight-question index of organizational commitment, and on turnover intention, as measured in a single question: "How likely is it that you will try hard to find a job in another organization within the next 12 months?" They find that all employees at firms that offer child care benefits (not just on-site child care) are more committed to the firm and are significantly less likely to say that they intend to quit.

As has been noted in the literature reviews of studies attempting to measure the relationship between employee benefits and employment outcomes and costs, inadequate data and insufficiently rigorous research methodologies have made it difficult to definitively establish a link between ESCC and enhanced productivity, even as measured through its proxies (Rubin et al. 1989; Friedman 1987; Miller 1984; Williams and MacDermid 1994). Problems often cited include small sample size, the absence of data from before the program was implemented, the lack of an appropriate comparison group, the problem of the self-selection of employees into the program, and the difficulty in identifying the source of change when firms offer a large variety of employee benefits, many of which are aimed at easing work/family conflict. These problems are difficult to overcome, making the evaluation of ESCC a challenging research task.

In this study, we propose two very different approaches to analyzing the value of ESCC. The first approach, as discussed in Chapter 5, is to look at who uses on-site center care in two manufacturing firms that have such a center. Employee use of on-site center care is compared to use of center-based child care by employee parents at another manufacturing firm in the same industry and general vicinity that does not have an on-site center. We find that employees at the companies with on-site centers are much more likely to use center care than are employees at the company without an on-site center. Because the costs of the on-site care are similar to the average cost of paid day care in the area, we argue that our finding is evidence of the value of "on-siteness" and "employer sponsorship," and of the perceived benefit of center care more generally.

The second strategy for measuring the value of the benefit of an on-site center is to simply ask employees the value that they receive (or would receive) from an actual (or hypothetical) on-site center using the contingent valuation technique. The contingent valuation methodology (CVM) is explained in detail in Chapter 6, and the CVM results from the employees of the three manufacturing firms are examined in Chapter 7. One of the advantages of this approach is that it allows us to observe the value of the benefit to non-users in addition to users. In keeping with Grover and Crooker's (1995) results, we find that non-users, as well as users, ascribe substantial benefits to being employed by a firm that sponsors an on-site center.

The strategies we propose for studying the value of ESCC add to the menu of techniques available to researchers and to the firms themselves. The contingent valuation technique can be used by any mid- or large-sized firm, whether or not it has an on-site center. In addition, this strategy can be used to value other family-responsive policies. Observing parental usage of on-site centers is also important for understanding the value parents ascribe to "on-siteness" and "employer sponsorship" because these are qualities that only an employer or set of employers can provide. Given the increased demands on parents' time, convenience and reliability, in addition to quality, are predicted to be important attributes, which parents will "shop" for as they choose child care.

Notes

1. See Chapter 8 for further discussion of the government's role in the provision of child care in the United States.
2. This is quite different from health insurance, where there are clear cost advantages of increasing the size of the risk pool.
3. See Connelly and Kimmel (2003) for a recent review of this literature.
4. An alternative way of calculating the wage savings to the firm would be to sum individual employee values of the ESCC. In a perfectly competitive labor market, where each worker is paid the value of his or her marginal revenue product, the value of the employer-provided benefit to the worker results in a direct wage savings to the firm, equal in amount to the employee's valuation of the benefit (Summers 1989). However, if firms offer compensation through a broadly known wage structure in which all workers in the same category receive the same wages, and

in which a hierarchical wage scale is maintained, then individual workers' wages will not be discounted by their own valuation of the ESCC.

5. Some caution is needed in interpreting the results as the response rate in this study was only 28 percent.

4
Description of Study Sites and Data Collection

DESCRIPTION OF INDUSTRY AND FIRMS

The three firms included in our study produce essentially the same goods, using the same technology, and are each located within a relatively small geographic area surrounding a mid-sized city in the Southeast of the United States. The three firms are all in the same Standard Metropolitan Statistical Area (SMSA) and are within 20 miles or less of each other. The industry can best be characterized as light manufacturing, with the majority of the workforce having at most a high school education. The majority of nonmanagerial workers in the industry are women, although there are specific steps of the production process, such as loading, that are staffed primarily by men. Most of the production workers are paid by the piece, rather than according to an hourly wage rate. In recent years, many firms in the industry, including those studied here, experimented with a team-based production wage where two or three workers are paid for their joint output. Our discussions with employees suggest that, overall, both workers and managers are satisfied with this approach, and the firms continue to use it in some situations.

The majority of U.S. companies in the industry are concentrated in or near this SMSA. The domestic industry still manufactures the bulk of the products sold in the United States but struggles with growing competition from abroad. The industry faces increasing pressure from the wholesale buyers of its products as consumer demand and the nature of the retail market have changed. The regional labor market is also highly competitive. Real hourly wages in this state for production workers in the industry increased gradually but steadily during the 1990s, from about $8.20 to about $9.30. These average real wages were consistently higher than those for the comparable industry classification nationally. The unemployment rate in the state tends to be lower than the national level, with the rate in this region of the state lower still. For example, in 1998 the national unemployment rate was 4.5 percent, the unemployment rate in the state was 3.5 percent, and in the SMSA where the industry is concentrated (and our three firms are located), the rate was 2.7 percent (U.S. Department of Labor 2002). The forces of greater foreign competition, decreasing consumer demand, increased market power of retailers, and an extremely tight labor market have combined to create a sense of a struggle to survive in the industry; firms are always looking for innovations that will help them to meet their demand for labor and maintain or strengthen their competitive position in the global market. Such innovations take many forms, including the adoption of new technology, restructuring of work times, and considering alternative packages of employee benefits.

There are approximately 60 firms in this industry in our study area, and the industry is one of the primary employers in the region. Only 2 of the 60 firms have on-site child care, both of which are included in the study. No other firms offer any type of child care benefit, although several have considered doing so. Firms in the industry range in size from a maximum of about 800 employees to fewer than 50. All three firms studied here are larger than the average firm in the industry, allowing us to gather sufficient information for multivariate statistical analysis. At the time of our surveys, Action Industries had a workforce of about 600, Bell Manufacturing had about 300 employees, and Central Products had about 640 employees.[1] Action and Bell had on-site child care centers and Central did not.

Action Industries and Central Products are family-held companies. Bell Manufacturing had recently gone public at the time of our interviews, although the child care center had been established before this. Each company offers a modest set of benefits that includes a 401(k) retirement plan and health insurance. Workers do not receive any paid sick time or flexible vacation time. Each company shuts down for a companywide vacation, typically for two weeks a year, and workers receive their average earnings for those two weeks. Action also offers flextime to its workers, and a subsidized fitness center and cafeteria. Bell offers some employees flextime and a slightly discounted participation in community center fitness programs. Central has a subsidized cafeteria, short-term disability insurance, and some flexibility in the scheduling of work hours. These benefits packages, except for the child care centers, are similar to those available at other large companies in the industry. The smaller firms generally have less generous 401(k) matching and lower quality health insurance. Regarding wages, because most workers are paid "by the piece" and piece rates vary within the firm from one product to another, it is difficult to derive an exact comparison of wages across firms. However, workers and management alike reported their perception that wages were very similar across firms in this industry. Central's human resource officer indicated concern over the possibility that workers might leave his company for another in the industry in response to a very small difference in wages. Action and Bell administrators reported being less concerned about small differences in wages, feeling that the on-site center provided them some cushion. Still, at each firm we encountered employees who had worked at several other firms in the area.

Because the three firms are located in the same geographic area, employees with young children face the same market options for child care (e.g., large day care centers, individuals who run small child care facilities in their homes, and professional in-home care providers). Parents, however, differ substantially in their access to low- or zero-priced care by relatives and in their eligibility for state government child care subsidies. In addition, of course, those working for Action Industries or Bell Manufacturing have an on-site center available to them.

DESCRIPTION OF ESCC CENTERS

The descriptions of the Action and Bell on-site child care centers reflect conditions at the time of data collection (1996 for Action and 1997 for Bell). Information about ESCC at each firm was obtained from interviews with the directors of the child care centers and the chief human resource officers, from company literature about the centers, and from direct observation of each center. The on-site child care center at Action Industries opened in 1979 and had about 80 children enrolled at the time of the survey. The owner of the company told us that he started the day care center in order to attract women employees in a very tight labor market. He recalled the unemployment rate being quite low in 1979, when the company began manufacturing the product instead of simply wholesaling it. He indicated that it was a fairly impulsive decision, not one subject to detailed cost-benefit analysis, but a choice to which he remains committed and to which he attributes much of his business success.

Action's child care center charged a set rate per preschool child (ages six weeks through five years) for full-time care during the work week, with some discounting for multiple children: $47.50 per week for the first child, $86.50 per week for two children (a discount of $4.25 per child, per week), and $112.00 per week for three children (a discount of $10.17 per child, per week). Part-time care during the work week was also available. Its hours of operation were from 6:00 a.m. to 6:00 p.m., Monday through Friday. These hours straddle the work time of first-shift workers, who have some degree of flexibility in their individual starting and ending times. In addition to providing part-time or full-time care for preschool children, the center also offered after-school and "snow day" care for children aged 6 to 13. There are several indicators of relatively high quality of care at Action Industries compared to other center-based facilities in the area. For example, the ratio of children to care providers is lower for each age group than required by state regulations, and the child care providers are paid at a higher rate than average for such workers in the area. There was a waiting list for the children of 10 employees for the on-site center at Action at the time of the survey. Parent fees do not fully cover the operating costs of the child care center, and the space and maintenance of the facility are provided by the firm at no cost. Action Industries estimates that it subsidizes almost 50 percent of the total cost of the center, which at the time of the survey was a subsidy of about $130,000 per year.

The Bell Manufacturing child care center opened in 1989 and had 60 children under six years of age enrolled at the time of the survey. There was some sense among administrators with whom we spoke that Bell's rationale for opening the center was to better compete with Action Industries for workers, although the owner of Action was consulted by the owners of Bell during the process of establishing the center. According to Action's owner, "We did help them [Bell] develop it [the on-site center]; they are good friends of ours. They have expanded it to the point where it's about the same size as we have." The labor market in the area at the time Bell opened its center was even tighter than in the late 1970s, with state unemployment rates of 3.6 percent for

1988 and 3.5 percent for 1989, compared to 5.5 and 5.3 percent nationally for these years (U.S. Department of Labor 2002). The Bell center charged a set rate per preschool child of $49 for full-time care with a 5 percent discount for the second and third children. Saturday care was available at the time of the survey. Its hours of operation were Monday through Friday, 5:45 a.m. to 5:30 p.m. (35 percent of Bell employees report having flextime, with the first shift beginning between 6:00 and 8:00 a.m.), and also on Saturday while a shift was working. Like that at Action Industries, the Bell Manufacturing center is a relatively high quality facility based on lower child/staff ratios than required by law and a high level of staff education. Child care providers are full-time employees of the company, receiving higher pay than other providers in the area and full benefits. At Bell, there was a waiting list for the children of three employees at the time of the survey. Bell reported subsidizing the center at about the same percentage rate as Action, or by as much as $100,000 per year at the time of the survey. The Bell Center also was receiving $25,000 from the federal food stamp program a year and about $20,000 a year over a four-year period from the state child care quality enhancement fund. The director reported that the center occasionally enrolled children from the community. These children were charged $20 more per week, reflecting the firm's public statement of the level of subsidy.

The third firm, Central Products, does not have an on-site child care center. As previously discussed, Central's benefits package is somewhat more generous than average among the companies in the area, but it is similar to that of Action Industries and Bell Manufacturing. At the time of our survey in 1998 (and still today), Central was not interested in sponsoring a child care center, or in subsidizing child care more generally. The human resource officer at Central indicated that he felt very confident that the firm's benefits dollars are better spent elsewhere, such as for short-term disability insurance. Many of his employees disagreed and spoke about the important benefit that could be gained from an on-site child care center. Central Products, therefore, serves as an ideal comparison case to firms with on-site centers for the analysis of the type of child care selected by working parents and for the assessment of the value of an employer-sponsored on-site center.

DESCRIPTION OF DATA COLLECTION

Data collection took place during the summers of 1996, 1997, and 1998, with the employees of one firm interviewed each year. Interviews with individual employees were conducted in person at each firm on company time, during every work shift and drawing from all departments. This strategy was selected in order to maximize participation given budget and time constraints, while achieving a high degree of representativeness of workers. We interviewed approximately 60 percent of the workforce at Action Industries, 75 percent at Bell Manufacturing, and 65 percent at Central Products, which, in each case, represented our data collection capacity given the time constraints of the firms, and nearly universal participation of targeted employees.

The survey instrument was highly comparable across firms, with minimal tailoring by site to take into account firm-specific characteristics, and with slight changes made from one firm to the next in order to benefit from insights gained at each company. Each survey collected detailed socioeconomic and demographic information about the employee, the employee's spouse or partner (if applicable), and demographic data about the employee's household. For those employees with children under age 13, information was collected on the primary and secondary child care arrangements during the employee's normal work times, as well as on the type of care if the employee worked overtime on Saturdays. For the purposes of this analysis, we concentrate on children under six years old. In addition, questions were asked about alternative sources of child care in the area, including the availability of relatives and friends to care for one's child. Cost information was collected for each type of child care used, and respondents were asked about anticipated costs of alternative sources of care.

Table 4.1 highlights selected characteristics of respondents at each of the three firms (more detailed descriptive statistics are provided in Chapters 5 and 7). The employees at the three firms are quite similar in terms of being predominantly female, White Caucasian, and without any college education. They are also of a comparable age and are similar in the percentage with young children. There are some interesting differences across firms in the distribution of racial and ethnic groups and in the percentage of employees who are male. The two are some-

Table 4.1 Selected Demographic Characteristics of Employees at the Three Firms Surveyed

	Action Industries	Bell Manufacturing	Central Products
On-site child care center	Yes	Yes	No
% male	19.6	25.1	32.1
Race/ethnicity			
% Hispanic	0.0	4.5	0.0
% African American	4.5	15.1	5.9
% Hmong	9.9	0.0	21.4
% White Caucasian	83.7	80.4	70.7
% other	1.9	0.0	2.0
Mean age (years)	35.7	38.1	37.0
% with children under 6 years old	33.3	24.6	27.0
Mean number of children under 6 years old	0.45	0.29	0.40
% with college degree	7.1	3.5	2.0
Number of employees in sample	312	199	393

what correlated given that Central Products has the largest proportion of Hmong workers, and Hmong men are doing some of the jobs in the factory that have been traditionally filled by women. The large Hmong presence also contributes to the somewhat greater percentage of workers at Central Products and Action Industries with children under the age of six, and the substantially greater mean number of young children at these two firms. The Hmong marry quite young, often at 13 or 14 years of age for women, and have very high fertility. We talked with a number of young Hmong women, aged 18 to 21, with four or five children already. Excluding the Hmong, the mean number of children under age six in our three samples is 0.36, 0.29, and 0.22, respectively, consistent with arguments about the recruitment and retention potential of ESCC among workers with young children.

The large Hmong presence at Action Industries and Central Products is somewhat problematic for our statistical analysis of child care arrangements in that Hmong parents have a very strong cultural preference for care by relatives for their children. Despite their employment at Action, no Hmong children (out of 43 under the age of six) are enrolled in the on-site center. Hmong parents rely almost exclusively on splitting shifts to provide care for their large families. In most cases, the father works the first shift, and the mother works the second shift. This is not the only pattern, but it seems to be the preferred one. Nearly 70 percent of Hmong children of employees at Central and 40 percent of Hmong children of employees at Action are cared for by their father while their mother is at work. Most of the remaining Hmong preschool children are cared for by grandparents and other relatives. Aside from two Hmong children in center care (but not the on-site center) at Action, the Hmong children we studied were not cared for at a center or even by a nonrelative.

Because of these strong cultural preferences, Chapter 5 analyzes the child care arrangements of only the non-Hmong employees of all three firms. However, we include Hmong employees in the analysis in Chapter 7. They are, of course, employees of the firms and are expected to have a very different valuation of ESCC as a benefit in comparison to other employees. The fact that we find the estimated willingness to pay for an on-site center among the Hmong to be substantially less than the average for the non-Hmong sample is one piece of evidence that our contingent valuation methodology is yielding reasonable results.

A critical part of the survey at each firm was the section that elicited information about the value that employees place on the existing or hypothetical on-site child care center (the contingent valuation questions). The structure of this part of the survey is discussed in detail in Chapter 6. Here we note only that the design of the contingent valuation questions, as well as that of other parts of the survey, was informed by preliminary fieldwork at each company. The fieldwork consisted of focus group discussions with a small number of workers, interviews with representatives of management, and pre-testing of actual survey questions. In particular, great care was taken both in the construction and the implementation of the survey to ensure that respondents understood the contingent valuation questions, which are more complex than most survey questions.

A weakness of the data lies in the relatively small sample size for multivariate analysis and in the fact that only three firms in one industry and in one local labor market are represented. While we recognize this limitation, we believe that the unique features of the data are of sufficient interest to outweigh this drawback. The method we use for the valuation of on-site child care to employees might be adopted by a single firm interested in optimizing benefit dollars. In addition, it is important to recall that rarely do we have the opportunity to analyze on-site child care except through a case study approach, given its low incidence in the general population and the ordinary sample sizes of representative household surveys about child care.

Note

1. In order to preserve confidentiality, we use fictitious names for the three firms.

5

Analysis of the Use
of Employer-Sponsored
On-Site Child Care

It is good for parents to have kids close by.

Still couldn't get service for less elsewhere.

Convenience of location.

Trust people.
　　　　　—Employee comments about the value of the on-site center

This chapter addresses the following question: Does the presence of an employer-sponsored on-site child care center have an impact on parental decisions about child care? As such, the analysis focuses on the child care choices of employees with young children at the three study sites.[1] We see this research as an indirect approach to assessing the value that workers receive from the availability of an on-site ESCC center. If parents value the "on-siteness" of the center or its "employer-sponsoredness," then they may choose it over other child care options, including other center settings, of comparable or even lower price. We know from other sources that parents value convenience and quality of child care arrangements (Sonenstein 1991). Given the descriptions of the centers in the previous chapter, and the numerous comments from employees such as those quoted above, it seems reasonable that parents would find ESCC to be both convenient and of high quality.

Our findings show a substantial difference in the usage patterns of alternative child care modes between the two firms with on-site child care centers and the one firm without an on-site center. More than 40 percent of the employees with young children at Action Industries and Bell Manufacturing have children enrolled in the on-site centers. The child care category receiving many fewer children from Action and Bell is home-based day care provided by nonrelatives (family day care). This is in keeping with other research, which shows that family day care is the category most identified with employment-facilitating child care, while center care is also viewed as providing education or social interaction for young children (Connelly and Kimmel 2003; Davis and Connelly 2003). We further find that infants are as likely as older children to be enrolled in the on-site centers. Studies of child care choice usually find that infants are less likely than older children to be enrolled in center care (Connelly and Kimmel 2003; Davis and Connelly 2003; Han 1999; Lehrer 1983; Lehrer 1989). Our conclusion is that these national results are, in part, a reflection of availability rather than of parental preferences since parents in our study with the option of enrolling infants in the on-site center do so. The finding that infants are as likely as older children to be enrolled in the on-site center may additionally reflect the unique features of on-site centers over community-based ones in that parents can more easily see their children during the day and that the center has the company "seal of approval." Our results also suggest that those using the on-site centers represent a broad range of workers and are not limited to highly educated, salaried employees, and that users of the on-site center are less likely to need secondary child care arrangements.

The rest of the chapter proceeds as follows. We first present a descriptive analysis of the primary child care arrangements of employees with young children by firm, comparing the distribution of arrangements to a nationally representative sample and comparing the employees who work at firms with on-site child care to those who work at the firm without this benefit. We consider the role of alternative child care options and the price of such alternatives relative to the price of the one chosen. This is followed by a discussion of secondary care arrangements that focuses on differences associated with access to on-site child care. Systematic information on "back-up" child care plans is not widely available for the United States; thus, this part of the descriptive analysis is important even without the consideration of on-site care. The remainder of the chapter uses a multivariate model to analyze the determinants of the use of on-site child care by employees with young children at Action Industries and Bell Manufacturing, and the use of any center-based care by employees at Central Products. We estimate the model for each firm separately, as well as a model for the use of any type of center-based child care for the employees at the three firms combined, controlling for fixed firm effects.

PRIMARY ARRANGEMENTS

> *A lot of people don't have any other choice but Child View [Bell's on-site center].*
>
> *The on-site center is more convenient and cost effective for single parents.*
>
> —Bell Manufacturing employees' responses as to why they voted yes to being willing to help pay for an employer-sponsored on-site child care center

Like parents throughout the United States, the manufacturing workers in our study who are parents of young children use a variety of child care arrangements. Within this range of choices, it is clear that when an on-site child care center is available to these employees the distribution of primary child care arrangements looks quite different than when ESCC is not available. Table 5.1 compares the primary type of care arrangements used for young children of employed non-Hmong mothers at the three factories to the national averages we reported on more fully in Chapter 2.[2] This table is limited to children under age five of women employees to make our data more comparable to national statistics, which are based on all children under age five with full-time employed mothers during the spring of 1997.[3]

In thinking about the impact of an on-site center on parental choice of child care, we use Central Products employees as representative of women factory workers in the area because the vast majority of manufacturing workers do not have access to on-site day care. Thus, we begin our analysis by comparing the child care arrangements of the children of non-Hmong Central employees (column 3) to the national averages (column 4).[4] That comparison suggests that the distribution of care arrangements used for children of employees of a manufacturing firm in a midsized Southeastern city is quite similar to that used for children of employed mothers nationwide. Non-Hmong mothers at Central rely slightly more heavily on grandparents and relatives and less on nonrelatives than do mothers nationally. This difference is, in part, because of their relatively low incomes, as child care provided by grandparents and relatives tends to be a less expensive option. It is also, in part, because of the greater availability of grandparents and rel-

Table 5.1 Distribution of Primary Type of Child Care Used by Non-Hmong Employed Mothers with Children under Age Five

Primary type of child care used by employed mothers	Action Industries 1996	Bell Manufacturing 1997	Central Products 1998	National statistics, full-time employed mothers 1997
Any child care center	80.5	66.7	30.8	27.0
(On-site center)	(65.9)	(41.0)		—
Spouse or child's other parent in your home	3.7	2.6	15.4	15.8
Grandparent	12.2	23.1	20.6	19.1
Relative	0.0	2.6	10.2	8.3
Nonrelative	3.7	5.1	20.5	25.3
At school	0.0	0.0	2.6	2.1
Mother cares for child at work	0.0	0.0	0.0	1.3
Number in sample	82	39	39	—

NOTE: Firm samples for this table are limited to children under age five of employed mothers to make them comparable with national statistics. For Action Industries, 18 children have been dropped from the sample because their father is the Action Industries employee. For Bell Manufacturing, 12 children have been dropped for this reason, and at Central Products, 17 children have been dropped. National statistics are from the U.S. Census Bureau (2002a) and are weighted to be nationally representative. The national sample does not exclude Hmong mothers, but they constitute a very small percentage of the total population. Blank cell = not applicable. — = not available.
SOURCE: U.S. Census Bureau (2002b).

atives in this area, where most grown children do not move very far away from their parents.[5]

We now compare column 3 with columns 1 and 2, which represent the distribution of child care arrangements used by employed mothers at Action Industries and Bell Manufacturing, where on-site child care is available. The most striking difference among these columns is the use of center care. At Action, 80.5 percent of preschool children of non-Hmong women employees are enrolled in center care, either at the on-site day care center or at some other center. The vast majority of center users (82 percent) are at the on-site center, with 10 more children of Action employees in our sample on the waiting list at the time of our survey.[6] Similarly, two-thirds of children of Bell Manufacturing women employees are enrolled in center care, either at the Bell day care center or at another center. Again, the majority of center users are at the on-site facility (61 percent), and there was also a waiting list for the Bell center. This compares with 30.8 percent of non-Hmong Central Products children and 27.0 percent nationally at center-based care.

With such a large percentage of children cared for in the on-site centers, it is interesting to see which arrangements are less common for the children of Action Industries and Bell Manufacturing workers. While the use of other center-based care is still substantial among the workers of these two firms, it is less heavily relied upon at Action than at Central Products or nationally. Thus, to some extent, on-site child care replaces other forms of center-based child care. However, the use of other center-based care is not the only category of care that is diminished when on-site child care is available. Grandparent care for Bell employees is not noticeably diminished compared to Central employees, but Action employees are less likely to use grandparents as caregivers. Action and Bell mothers are also less likely to use father care, relative care other than grandparents, and are much less likely to use nonrelatives than are Central mothers. These three categories seem to be less preferred when affordable, convenient center-based care is available.[7]

It is important to note that the center care at Action Industries and Bell Manufacturing, while subsidized by the firms, is not inexpensive. Table 5.2 shows the mean weekly amount paid for care at both centers. The average reported weekly expenditure among Action Industries on-site users is $49.58 and at Bell Manufacturing is $37.51. While this is less than the weekly expenditures for other center-based care in the area, non-Hmong parents using child care other than center care pay substantially less per week. Action parents not using the on-site center pay $30.57 on average, while Bell parents pay $25.62, and Central Products parents pay $30.94 per week. This substantial difference in costs is largely the result of the percentage of non-on-site users who are using care arrangements with no money cost. Once we omit those not paying for care, the amount paid is much more similar across columns. The Bell on-site center seems, at first glance, to be priced "below-market," but this average is somewhat misleading. As will be discussed

Table 5.2 Characteristics of Child Care for Non-Hmong Employees' Children under Age Six

	Action Industries		Bell Manufacturing		Central Products
	On-site users[a]	Non-users[b]	On-site users[a]	Non-users[b]	
Mean weekly amount paid per child for care (including zeroes)	$49.58 (8.34)	$30.57 (30.71)	$37.51 (17.03)	$25.62 (32.65)	$30.94 (32.47)
% paying for care	100.00	59.09	100.00	51.28	60.87
Mean weekly amount paid per child for care by those who pay	$49.58 (8.34)	$51.73 (21.98)	$37.51 (17.03)	$54.44 (25.92)	$50.83 (26.69)
Mean weekly amount paid per child for center care	$49.58 (8.34)	$53.22 (20.26)	$37.51 (17.03)	$71.37 (24.31)	$68.76 (29.84)
Mean age of children (years)	2.33 (1.46)	2.80 (1.68)	3.03 (1.56)	2.85 (1.50)	3.08 (1.55)
Satisfaction ranking of parents towards their child's primary care arrangement (1 is the best ranking, 5 the worst)	—	—	median: 1 mean: 1.67 (1.20)	median: 1 mean: 1.81 (1.02)	median: 2 mean: 2.20 (1.44)
Number of children	63	49	26	39	71

NOTE: Standard deviations are in parentheses. Children enrolled in primary school are excluded. — = not available.
[a] In this and subsequent tables, the term "On-site users" refers to users of the on-site child care center.
[b] "Non-users" refers to those using some form of child care other than the on-site center.

more fully, many users of the on-site center at Bell Manufacturing receive a state government subsidy for child care, unlike the case at Action Industries. Judging from the data, some of the recipients of the subsidy reported their out-of-pocket cost of child care, net of the state subsidy, rather than the total charged by the center. When this difference is taken into account, the average charge per child at the two on-site centers is almost identical. Thus, the price of the on-site centers is about equal to the local market rates for paid child care in general but is somewhat lower than the local rate for other center-based care.[8]

Because the on-site center is not an inexpensive form of child care, the question arises as to why so many parents use it. Some of the parents using the on-site center do not have a zero- or low-cost option, and thus the on-site center offers roughly the same price as other paid options, a more convenient location, and at minimum, an acceptable level of quality. On the other hand, some of the parents using the on-site center do have a zero- or low-cost option but choose the center as being more convenient, more reliable (in terms of the arrangement not breaking down), and perhaps of higher quality.[9]

Table 5.3 compares employees with young children across firms in terms of the availability of alternative caregivers and the amount expected to pay those caregivers. Based on the percentage of employees with parents or parents-in-law in the area, on-site center users do not seem to differ from users of other arrangements. In fact, on-site users at both Action Industries and Bell Manufacturing are slightly more likely to have parents in the area. Many studies of child care arrangements use the presence of parents or parents-in-law in the area as an indicator of a zero-cost child care alternative. Substantially fewer on-site users at both Action and Bell report having parents or parents-in-law who are available for child care. This provides some evidence that many users of the on-site center do not have a zero- or low-cost option available to them, although one wonders if more grandparents would be available if the need were greater, i.e., if there were no on-site center.[10] Still, taking the data at face value, 19 percent of the users of the Action center and 38 percent of the users of the Bell center report having a zero-cost alternative child care arrangement available to them. Clearly, some parents are choosing the on-site center over other care arrangements despite a relatively high price tag. Convenience and reliability are likely to be factors in parents' choice of the on-site center;

Table 5.3 Child Care Options of Non-Hmong Employees with Children under Age Six

	Action Industries		Bell Manufacturing		Central Products
	On-site users	Non-users	On-site users	Non-users	
% with parents in area	83.33	63.33	80.95	71.88	81.82
% of parents available for care of those in the area	17.14	63.16	35.29	69.57	53.33
% who expect to pay for grandparent care	25.00	8.33	16.67	13.33	58.82
Range of expected payments per week	$35–45	$25	$40	$40	$25–150
% with other relatives in area	55.26	53.85	80.95	46.88	64.81
% of other relatives available for care of those in the area	28.57	35.71	41.18	33.33	48.57
% who expect to pay for relative care	20.00	20.00	57.14	0.00	75.00
Range of expected payments per week	$65	$25	$35–90		$20–70
% who know others (nonrelatives) available for care	24.44	46.67	23.81	28.12	30.91
% who expect to pay for nonrelative care	100.00	40.00	50.00	100.00	75.00
Range of expected payments per week	$18–75	$45–50	$20–40	$45–60	$20–200

% who know of any child care centers	56.25	57.14	71.43	50.00	60.00
% who expect to pay for center care	100.00	100.00	100.00	.	100.00
Range of expected payments	$35-92	$25-125	$10-100	$72-155	$58-100
% with zero-cost care option (not including spouse)	18.75	37.14	38.10	31.25	18.18
Number of employees	48	35	21	32	55

NOTE: Children enrolled in primary school are excluded. Employees whose grandchild or other relative is enrolled in the on-site center are excluded. Two grandparents are excluded from the Action Industries sample, and three employees, two grandparents and an aunt, are excluded from the Bell Manufacturing sample. Blank cell = not applicable.

quality or a preference for center care may also be reasons for choosing the on-site center.

Thinking further about parental preferences across a set of child care options, we return to Table 5.2 to see that Bell parents are happier in general with their arrangements than are Central parents, as indicated by both the median and mean scores.[11] There is no difference between the median level of satisfaction of on-site center users and other parents at Bell; however, the mean score indicates somewhat greater satisfaction with the on-site center than with other child care arrangements. In addition, Table 5.2 shows that the mean age of the children at the on-site centers is not markedly greater than the mean age of children in other arrangements. General research on the mode of child care choice among employed mothers in the United States has found that parents are more likely to use relative care for very young children and center-based care for older preschool children (Chaplin et al. 1996; Connelly and Kimmel 2003; Hofferth and Wissoker 1992; Waite, Leibowitz, and Witsberger 1991). It has never been clear, however, whether this lower probability of using center-based care for very young children represented parental preferences or the lack of infant care slots in day care centers. Here, at least for on-site center-based care, there does not appear to be a parental preference for older children relative to younger children to be in center-based care, or for younger children to not be in center-based care. This conclusion is further supported by the fact that, among sample users of the Action Industries and Bell Manufacturing centers combined, there are 19 families with two preschool-aged children including 17 that use the on-site center for both children. In contrast, 23 percent of a national sample of center users from the 1994 SIPP data follow the pattern suggested by other child care researchers of using home-based or relative care for the younger child and center-based care for the older child. No family in our samples of on-site center users follows this pattern. There seems to be no shying away from on-site center care for younger children among the parents at Action and Bell, nor is there any evidence of a strong preference for relative or home-based care for younger children at any of the three firms.[12]

SECONDARY ARRANGEMENTS

We also asked questions about a second regular child care arrangement for each of the four youngest children in a family, as the literature on child care in the United States has emphasized the cobbled-together plans many parents use to provide sufficient care for their children while they are at work (see Table 5.4). Again, focusing on children under age six, at Action Industries, 9.8 percent of children enrolled in the on-site center have regular secondary child care arrangements, compared with 28.3 percent of the non-on-site center users. No secondary arrangements of on-site center users involve a money transfer, while 36.4 percent of the secondary arrangements of non-on-site users involve payment, ranging from $10 to $50 per week. Although the number of cases is small, the difference suggests that the on-site center reduces the need to maintain two sets of arrangements.

Table 5.4 Secondary Arrangements for Children under Age Six of Bell Manufacturing and Central Products Non-Hmong Employees

| | Action Industries | | Bell Manufacturing | | |
	On-site users	Non-users	On-site users	Non-users	Central Products
% with regular secondary care	9.8	28.3	11.5	47.4	46.3
Type of secondary care:	—	—			
% center			0.0	0.0	9.7
% spouse			33.3	27.8	6.5
% grandparent			33.3	38.9	29.0
% relative			33.3	16.7	38.7
% nonrelative			0.0	0.0	16.1
% sibling			0.0	11.1	0.0
% enrolled in primary school			0.0	5.6	0.0
Level of satisfaction	—	—	median: 1 mean: 1.0 (0.0)	median: 2 mean: 2.4 (1.7)	median: 1 mean: 2.1 (1.6)
% pay for secondary care	0.0	36.4	0.0	29.4	25.8
Number of children	62	38	26	39	71

NOTE: Standard deviations are in parentheses for level of satisfaction. Children enrolled in primary school are excluded. — = not available.

At Bell Manufacturing and Central Products, we expanded the data collection on secondary arrangements to include the type of secondary arrangement and level of satisfaction. Comparing the on-site center users and non-users at Bell, we found the same pattern as at Action Industries, that on-site center users are much less likely to report maintaining regular secondary arrangements. No secondary arrangements of on-site center users involve a money transfer, while 29.4 percent of non-on-site center users who have secondary arrangements report paying for that arrangement, with payments ranging from $35 to $110 per week. Secondary arrangements used by Bell workers rely heavily on the other parent or spouse, grandparents, and other relatives. As was the case at Action, on-site center care at Bell seems to reduce the need for secondary arrangements, particularly paid secondary arrangements. This is beneficial to parents in that it reduces transaction costs and, in some cases, reduces monetary costs. The feedback from Bell employees also suggests that they are somewhat more satisfied with their primary arrangements than with their secondary arrangements. Thus, reducing the need for secondary care may increase parents' overall satisfaction with child care arrangements.

Without the benefit of an on-site center, 46 percent of Central Products children have a second regular child care arrangement. Central children who are in center-based care for their primary arrangement are just as likely as the full Central sample to have a regular secondary arrangement. This suggests that the on-site centers may be better than other centers at avoiding the need for a secondary arrangement. Of the secondary arrangements at Central, 74 percent are unpaid. Secondary arrangements used by Central employees are mainly with relatives, with about 7 percent of the secondary care provided by the employee's spouse, 29 percent provided by grandparents, and 39 percent provided by another relative.

COMPARISON OF EMPLOYEE CHARACTERISTICS

I didn't really visualize how important a role that [the on-site child care] would play in the company in terms of attracting management....You can look at the company now and I would think that the great majority of

middle level managers that we have today in accounting, marketing, human resources are women in their late twenties to early forties who are either continuing or just completing the child building part of their lives and I would think that many of them would have worked in other places if this benefit hadn't been available.
    —Owner of Action Industries

Tables 5.5a and 5.5b compare employee users of the on-site center with other employees who have young children and with employees with no children under the age of six for Action Industries and Bell Manufacturing, respectively. Table 5.5c compares the sample of Central employees with and without young children.

At both Action and Bell, users of the on-site child care center are overwhelmingly first-shift workers and are more likely than non-users to be married and female. On-site center users are also less likely to be hourly production workers than are non-users, being more heavily concentrated among child care workers. At Action, on-site center users also have a higher mean level of education, which reflects the fact that all 11 college graduates with young children whom we interviewed use the on-site center. These patterns notwithstanding, it is also important to note that almost all types of worker categories at Action and at Bell are represented among the users of ESCC.

A substantial difference appears between employees with children enrolled in the child care center and noncenter users in the number of years they have worked at Action Industries or at Bell Manufacturing. This may be indicative of reduced turnover of parents of young children who have access to on-site child care, or may simply reflect the fact that new employees often have to wait for a slot in the on-site center.[13] The mean job tenure of the parents of children on the waiting list at Action is 2.2 years, which is much more similar to the noncenter user group than the user sample. The job tenure of those on the waiting list at Bell is quite low, two-thirds of a year. Children on the waiting list are also a whole year younger than the average child at the center. Their recent birth may be the explanation of their waiting list status rather than their parent's job tenure.[14]

Another possible explanation for the difference in job tenure is that length of employment is related to shift. The child care center is overwhelmingly used by first-shift workers. If first-shift jobs, when they become open, are filled by second-shift workers, then first-shift

Table 5.5a Characteristics of Action Industries Non-Hmong Employees by Care Status of Children under Age Six[a]

	Employees with children who are on-site center users	Employees with children who are not on-site center users	Employees without children under age 6
Mean number of children under age 6	1.33 (0.48)	1.20 (0.47)	
Mean number of children aged 6 to 12	0.29 (0.54)	0.69 (0.76)	0.23 (0.48)
Mean hours worked per week	40.84 (4.38)	40.69 (4.21)	40.51 (3.66)
Mean level of education (years)	13.15 (2.08)	11.97 (1.18)	12.39 (1.92)
Category of worker			
% hourly office workers	14.58	0.00	15.09
% hourly production workers	12.50	40.00	33.49
% pieceworkers	52.08	54.29	32.08
% salaried workers	14.58	2.86	13.68
% child care workers	6.25	2.86	5.66
Time of day employed			
% 1st shift	93.75	71.43	70.75
% 2nd shift	0.00	2.86	4.72
% 3rd shift	6.25	25.71	24.53
Marital status			
% married	87.50	71.43	64.90
% widowed	0.00	0.00	1.92
% divorced	4.17	11.43	12.02
% separated	2.08	5.71	3.85
% never married	6.25	11.43	17.31
Mean age (years)	29.08 (4.96)	27.86 (4.24)	39.79 (11.37)
% female	87.50	77.14	80.66
Race/ethnicity			
% White	93.75	94.29	92.92
% African American	2.08	5.71	5.19
% other	4.17	0.00	1.89
Mean years at Action Industries	4.61 (4.27)	2.71 (2.74)	6.91 (6.47)

	Employees with children who are on-site center users	Employees with children who are not on-site center users	Employees without children under age 6
Mean years lived in area	20.57	22.74	30.05
	(11.15)	(10.07)	(16.06)
Miles from home to work	10.36	13.23	11.02
	(6.63)	(8.91)	(8.38)
Number of employees	48	35	212

NOTE: Standard deviations are in parentheses. Children enrolled in primary school are excluded. NA = not applicable.

[a] Two employees have grandchildren at the center. The characteristics of these two grandparent employees are excluded from the users column and included in the column. Blank cell = not applicable.

Table 5.5b Characteristics of Bell Manufacturing Non-Hmong Employees by Care Status of Children under Age Six[a]

	Employees with children who are on-site center users	Employees with children who are not on-site center users	Employees without children under age 6
Mean number of children under age 6	1.19 (0.51)	1.09 (0.30)	
Mean number of children aged 6 to 12	0.67 (0.58)	0.28 (0.58)	0.24 (0.63)
Mean hours worked per week	42.33 (2.99)	41.91 (3.00)	43.22 (5.06)
Mean level of education (years)	12.33 (1.28)	12.00 (1.59)	12.38 (1.64)
Category of worker			
% hourly office workers	10.00	9.68	10.56
% hourly production workers	30.00	38.71	39.13
% pieceworkers	50.00	48.39	37.89
% salaried workers	0.00	3.23	8.07
% child care workers	10.00	0.00	4.35
Time of day employed			
% 1st shift	95.24	75.00	85.28
% 2nd shift	0.00	25.00	9.20
% 3rd shift	4.76	0.00	5.52
Marital status			
% married	76.19	71.88	57.67
% widowed	0.00	0.00	6.13
% divorced	9.52	12.50	11.04
% separated	9.52	0.00	1.84
% never married	4.76	15.62	23.31
Mean age (years)	30.55 (6.03)	29.03 (5.63)	40.40 (13.28)
% female	85.71	65.62	75.32
Race/ethnicity			
% White	65.22	76.67	83.33
% African American	34.78	10.00	12.96
% Hispanic	0.00	13.33	3.70
Mean years at Bell Manufacturing	4.86 (4.60)	1.74 (2.65)	8.78 (11.74)

	Employees with children who are on-site center users	Employees with children who are not on-site center users	Employees without children under age 6
Mean years lived in area	23.05	15.31	29.81
	(12.86)	(10.96)	(18.13)
Miles from home to work	9.83	9.31	8.62
	(9.13)	(6.45)	(7.93)
Number of employees	23	30	162

NOTE: Standard deviations are in parentheses. Children enrolled in primary school are excluded. Blank cell = not applicable.

[a]Three of the children enrolled at the center are grandchildren or the employee's sibling's child. Those employees are included in the last column of this table.

Table 5.5c Characteristics of Central Products Non-Hmong Employees with and without Children under Age Six

	Employees with children under age 6	Employees without children under age 6
Mean number of children under age 6	1.24 (0.51)	
Mean number of children aged 6 to 12	0.44 (0.60)	0.17 (0.53)
Mean hours worked per week	40.53 (5.90)	40.67 (4.30)
Mean level of education (years)	12.22 (1.70)	11.65 (1.83)
Category of worker		
% hourly office workers	10.91	15.53
% hourly production workers	27.27	44.70
% pieceworkers	56.36	34.09
% salaried workers	5.45	5.68
Time of day employed		
% 1st shift	74.55	67.80
% 2nd shift	16.36	15.91
% 3rd shift	9.09	16.29
Marital status		
% married	61.82	59.09
% widowed	1.82	3.79
% divorced	12.73	12.88
% separated	9.09	3.79
% never married	14.55	20.45
Mean age (years)	28.71 (5.30)	41.63 (13.57)
% female	72.22	66.15
Race/ethnicity		
% White	85.45	89.77
% African American	10.91	6.44
% other	3.64	3.79
Mean years at Central Products	2.91 (4.25)	7.87 (10.09)
Mean years lived in area	19.97 (11.58)	29.65 (17.05)
Miles from home to work	13.66 (10.17)	10.89 (8.81)
Number of employees	55	264

NOTE: Standard deviations are in parentheses. Children enrolled in primary school are excluded. Blank cell = not applicable.

workers will have longer job tenure at the firm than second-shift workers, on average. However, not all second-shift workers want to work first shift. Third shift appears to be quite different from first and second; it is much more common among the sample of workers without young children.

At Bell Manufacturing, there were no Hmong workers. Instead, the ethnic composition of the entire sample of Bell employees includes Latin American migrants and is more heavily African American and slightly less White than at Action Industries. No Hispanic workers with young children at Bell use the on-site center, but African-American workers with young children do (Table 5.5b). One-third of the employees with children at the on-site center are African American; this percentage is much greater than their representation among employees as a whole. In part, this is due to the fact that 30 percent of the African-American employees have young children compared with only 23 percent of the non-African-American employees. In addition, two-thirds of African-American employees with children under age six have a child enrolled in the on-site center compared to 34 percent of the non-African Americans.

There are also interesting differences between employees at the three firms with and without young children. Comparing these samples we find that employees without young children are, on average, older than those with young children.[15] They are more likely to work third shift and they have substantially longer job tenure than the younger employees with small children; many have been with their company for more than 10 years. Workers without young children are much less likely to be piece-rate workers at all three firms. This is probably due to their longer job tenure as some may have moved into supervisory positions. Workers without young children are more likely to be widowed or never married, but many are married and have older children. Eighty percent of Action Industries workers overall have had children, compared with the 32 percent who currently have young children. The comparable numbers at Bell Manufacturing are 82 and 25 percent, and at Central Products, 75 and 27 percent. These numbers are important because they point to the potential for grandchildren who may currently be enrolled or may be enrolled in the future in the on-site center. As Action's owner explained,

> I guess that the way the company has grown, almost everybody has experienced it [the on-site child care center] in one form or another whether it be having their own child in there or having a relative's child in there. We have a lot of inbred families in this company. Everybody's got a niece or a nephew that's been through the child care center. We do allow grandchildren to be in there and you know that is where I qualify; my grandchild is there right now.

DETERMINANTS OF ON-SITE CENTER USE

The variables reported in Tables 5.5a, 5.5b, and 5.5c represent, in part, our expectations of the factors that might influence the choice to enroll one's child in an on-site center. Because many of these variables are related to one another, we estimate a multivariate model to predict the usage of the on-site center for families with young children from the two factories with on-site centers.[16] Sample sizes are small; thus we interpret the results with caution. Sample size is especially a concern in the case of Bell Manufacturing, making the results of that analysis suggestive at best.

Characteristics of the employee parents included in the analysis are the number of years with the company, whether the individual is an hourly production worker or a piece worker (salaried or hourly office worker is the omitted category),[17] whether the person works first shift, hours worked per week, miles the employee lives from the factory, race/ethnicity dummy variables, whether a relative is available for child care, the proportion of life the employee has lived in the area, years of schooling, and age, sex, and marital status dummy variables (currently married is the omitted category). At Bell Manufacturing we included two race/ethnicity dummies, African American and Hispanic, based mainly on the differences observed in Table 5.5b, while at Central Products we included a single African-American indicator.[18]

Our expectation is that first-shift workers are more likely to use the on-site center because the center's hours of operation more closely match that schedule.[19] The number of years a worker has been with the company is expected to have a positive effect on the probability of enrolling in the on-site center, as previously discussed. We expect hourly production workers and piece workers to be less likely to enroll their child because they tend to have lower incomes than salaried and office workers.[20] We anticipate that the greater the distance from home to the factory, the less likely the employee will be to use the on-site center because it would mean a longer commute for the child.

Whether the employee indicated that a relative is available for child care and the proportion of years the employee has lived in the area are both expected to lower the probability of center enrollment because they both increase the probability of alternative care opportunities. Years of schooling is included to test whether workers with higher education prefer center-based care. Education may also pick up effects of income. At Action, this variable is entered as a set of thresholds because the descriptive analysis suggests that college education is strongly correlated with the use of the on-site center. At Bell and Central, there were too few college graduates with young children in the sample to include an indicator for college graduation. Instead, for these firms we enter education as a continuous variable.

We had no prior expectation about the age of the worker, but we control for age in order to be able to observe the independent effect of job tenure on the dependent variable. We expect the probability of enrollment to be lower for male employees because there is a greater potential for a stay-at-home spouse. Controlling for sex, divorced and never-married employees may be less likely to enroll their child at the center because family income is potentially lower than for married employees. On the other hand, married employees have their spouse and potentially two sets of parents and relatives who are possible child care providers.[21] The net result of marital status is thus theoretically ambiguous.

We also include three characteristics specific to the child: the child's age, the presence of preschool siblings, and the presence of primary school-aged siblings. The inclusion of the child's age allows us to test the hypothesis that parents prefer center-based care for older preschool children. The presence of preschool siblings is included to test the hypothesis that greater child care cost encourages parents to seek forms of care that are less expensive than the on-site center. The presence of primary school-aged siblings may also increase the total financial burden of child care, perhaps leading to a lower probability of using center-based care.

The dependent variable for Action Industries and Bell Manufacturing is whether the child is enrolled at the on-site center. The analysis sample is limited to those children who are not categorized as "in school" given that eligibility for "in school" status is institutionally determined and not within the parents' choice set. The sample size for Action is 100 non-Hmong children of employees. At Bell Manufacturing, the sample includes 59 children of employees. Of these, six are dropped because they are Hispanic and that characteristic is a perfect predictor of non-on-site center arrangements.

Table 5.6, column 1, shows the results of the probit estimation for the non-Hmong children of Action Industries workers, while column 2 shows the results for the non-Hispanic children of Bell Manufacturing workers. Despite the small sample sizes, a substantial number of the variables are statistically significant. We focus our discussion of results here on those of greatest interest to the provision of on-site child care.[22] Considering first the variables related to the child's characteristics, most importantly, the age of the child does not significantly affect enrollment in the on-site center at either firm. This is consistent with the descriptive results and provides further evidence that parents do not necessarily prefer relative and home-based care for younger children, even after controlling for the presence of such relatives.

In terms of the employee characteristics, job tenure is a significant positive predictor of on-site center use at both firms. This indicates that the availability of this benefit lowers attrition of users and/or that the limited number of slots available in the center tends to favor those who have worked at the firm longer.[23] Controlling for job tenure, being a first-shift worker is not a significant predictor of center use for workers at either firm. This is somewhat surprising given the time of day that on-site care is provided, but suggests a value to the on-site center that extends beyond its ability to facilitate employment.

Other employee variables that are significant negative predictors of enrollment in the Action Industries on-site center include being an hourly production worker or a piece worker, having some high school or some college, and being never married. Each of these variables, as expected, reduces the probability that the employee's child is enrolled

Table 5.6 Determinants of the Use of On-Site Center Care or Any Center-Based Care for Non-Hmong Children under Age Six

Dependent variable	Action Industries (on-site center)	Bell Manufacturing (on-site center)	Central Products (any center)	Combined sample (any center)
Child				
Child's age	−0.018	0.082	−1.121	0.052
	(0.118)	(0.341)	(0.816)	(0.073)
Siblings < age 6	0.027	−4.883	−6.345**	0.014
	(0.396)	(3.078)	(3.002)	(0.251)
Siblings aged 6–12	−0.807*	9.005**	−4.376**	0.081
	(0.426)	(3.543)	(2.044)	(0.227)
Employee				
Age of employee	−0.028	0.071	−0.160	−0.013
	(0.036)	(0.102)	(0.102)	(0.021)
Male	−0.471	5.524*	−3.321	−0.591*
	(0.690)	(2.966)	(2.346)	(0.332)
African American		2.108	1.897	1.049**
		(2.733)	(1.576)	(0.418)
Years of school		0.922*	−0.122	0.138*
		(0.475)	(0.341)	(0.079)
Some high school	−5.278*			
	(3.111)			
High school graduate	−4.716			
	(3.141)			
Some college	−5.179*			
	(3.119)			

(continued)

Table 5.6 (continued)

Dependent Variable	Action Industries (on-site center)	Bell Manufacturing (on-site center)	Central Products (any center)	Combined sample (any center)
Divorced	-0.858 (0.652)	5.401* (2.984)	4.967* (2.564)	0.170 (0.307)
Never married	-1.226** (0.611)	0.885 (1.722)	5.184* (3.556)	-0.179 (0.321)
Relatives available	-0.350 (0.424)	-4.993** (2.431)	-3.249** (1.449)	-0.781** (0.215)
Time in area	-0.836 (0.570)	12.731** (4.946)	-2.748 (2.253)	0.041 (0.258)
Miles to work	-0.044* (0.025)	-0.059 (0.161)	-0.219* (0.115)	-0.022* (0.013)
1st shift	0.390 (0.446)	4.110 (2.966)	6.343* (3.347)	0.705** (0.292)
Job tenure	0.101* (0.061)	0.833** (0.383)	-0.562 (0.385)	0.020 (0.033)
Hourly production	-2.060** (0.826)	-2.138 (2.579)	3.004 (2.694)	-0.515 (0.366)
Pieceworker	-1.220* (0.659)	-0.646 (1.655)	-1.515 (1.617)	-0.233 (0.328)
Hours per week	-0.013 (0.073)	-0.067 (0.184)	0.120 (0.099)	0.010 (0.282)
Bell Manufacturing				-0.338 (0.287)

Central Products				−1.092 **
				(0.269)
Number of children in sample	100	53	64	222
Log-likelihood	−40.96	−11.12	−13.11	−99.57
Chi-squared	53.46**	50.76**	49.84**	105.57**

NOTE: Probit coefficients are shown with standard errors in parentheses. *Significant at the 0.10 level, **significant at the 0.05 level. Blank cell = not applicable. The children of Hispanic workers at Bell Manufacturing are excluded from the Bell sample, but are included in the combined sample. Children enrolled in primary school are excluded.

in the on-site center. The results for the pay type and education variables indicate that even though the on-site centers are used by a broad range of workers (indeed, the number of college educated workers at these firms is too small to warrant an on-site center), there is a greater tendency to use ESCC among those with higher education and in managerial and administrative positions. Again, this may reflect income effects as well as attitudes and preferences about nonfamily care and early childhood education. Notably not significant at Action is the variable representing the availability of relatives, suggesting that the on-site center may be preferable to relative care even though relative care is a lower-cost option.

At Bell Manufacturing, the level of education of the parent also has a positive effect on the probability of using the on-site center. However, being divorced increases the probability of enrolling one's child in the on-site center, while there was no effect of this variable at Action Industries. We return to a discussion of the effects of marital status when we consider the results for Central Products. Also in contrast to Action, having a relative available reduces the probability of using the on-site center at Bell. Thus, the qualities of the on-site center do not appear to be sufficiently valued at Bell to systematically outweigh the availability of no-cost family care.

DETERMINANTS OF ANY CENTER USE

At Central Products, where there is no on-site center, we estimate a model of the determinants of the choice to enroll a child in any center-based care. Based on the preceding descriptive analysis, we expect the determinants of center-based care to be different from the determinants of on-site center care. We hypothesize that the convenience of the on-site center and its "employer-sponsoredness" make it a very different choice from center care in general. Table 5.6, column 3, shows the determinants of enrolling a preschool non-Hmong child in center care for the children of Central employees. As for the other two firms, the sample is limited to children under six who are not enrolled in school. The explanatory variables are the same as in column 2.[24]

The age of the child, again, is not a significant determinant of the use of center care. The community child care centers in this area seem to have sufficient infant care slots, which is not the case in many other child care markets. In terms of the characteristics of the employee, first-shift workers are more likely to use center-based care, as expected, because of the time of day that most center-based care is available. Job tenure has no impact on the use of center care, a result which is important in its difference from the positive result at the other two firms. Neither of the arguments in support of a positive effect of job tenure on ESCC use—reduced turnover and waiting time—are applicable to other center-based care.[25] The other variables that are significant determinants of center-based care for the children of Central Products employees include the availability of a relative, which has a negative effect on center use, and whether the employee is divorced, which is a positive predictor of center care. The negative effect of the relatives variable is particularly important in contrast to the lack of any such effect at Action Industries. This suggests that, in general, for center-based care that is not on-site and employer-sponsored, its qualities are not sufficiently valued to outweigh the advantages of no-cost family care.

For both Bell Manufacturing and Central Products, the large positive effect of being divorced may be related to the availability of state-provided child care subsidies. At the time of the surveys, these state subsidies, which target low-income families, were available in only some counties. The subsidies are not exclusively for center-based care, but they seem heavily weighted toward such care.[26] Likewise, they are not limited to unmarried mothers, but, again, in our data they are heavily weighted toward unmarried mothers. We experimented with replacing the marital status variables with a variable indicating that the family receives these state subsidies. That variable is significantly positive at Central Products and Bell Manufacturing, and significantly negative at Action Industries, with all other results unchanged. These findings are consistent with those for the marital status variables. Twelve children in our sample at the Bell center receive the state subsidies compared with one at Action Industries. This is largely attributable to location, as Action draws a greater percentage of its workforce from a county not covered by the subsidy program at the time of our interviews. Taken together, these results suggest that there are negative effects of being never married or divorced on center use, almost certainly related to lower income, but that at Bell and Central these effects are offset by the increased likelihood of eligibility for county-specific child care subsidies.

The final column of Table 5.6 reports the estimation of a model of the determinants of using any center-based care arrangement for our entire sample. Here we have combined the data from the non-Hmong workers of all three firms to gain the advantage of larger numbers and to look at the effect of working for an employer with an on-site center. The dependent variable, the use of any center-based care arrangement, is the same variable that is used in column 3 for Central Products only. Because all the workers in these three firms live in the same general area, they face the same price for "market" child care. The actual price of child care each family faces differs in three ways: by the availability of a relative who is willing to care for their child, by the availability of a subsidized employer-based on-site child care center, and, for low-income employees, by whether they live in a county included in the state child care subsidies program. The model in column 4 controls for the first two effects through the inclusion of the availability of relatives variable and the firm dummies, and for the last effect, imperfectly, through the marital status dummies.

Not surprisingly, given the large differentials we saw in Table 5.1 in the use of center care across the three firms, the multivariate results in Table 5.6 show that non-Hmong workers at Central Products are significantly less likely to use center-based arrangements. With Action Industries as the omitted category, the variable indicating employment at Bell Manufacturing is not significant, meaning that the workers at Action and Bell are equally likely to use center-based care, all else held constant.

Families with relatives available are less likely to use center-based arrangements, consistent with the firm-specific results for Central Products and Bell Manufacturing. Higher education, again, whether entered with thresholds or continuously, is positively related to center use.[27] The other significant variables in the full sample are whether the parent works first shift, whether the parent is African American, miles from home to work, and the sex of the employee. First-shift workers, African Americans, and women employees are more likely to use center-based care, as are those workers who live close to their place of employment. Interesting for their nonsignificance are job tenure (where, again, the hypothesized effects are relevant only for ESCC), whether the worker is a production worker (suggesting that, in this industry and child care market, center-based care overall is not systematically more likely to be selected by salaried administrative and managerial workers), marital status (where the opposing effects have negated one another), and child's age (again, important for its difference from the finding of many national studies that child's age has a positive effect on the use of center-based child care).

Comparing columns 1, 2, 3, and 4, we have further suggestive evidence to support the hypothesis that on-site ESCC is a different option from other types of center-based care. The on-site center at Action Industries is not less likely to be used by families with other relatives available in comparison to Central Products where relatives have a negative effect on center use. At both firms with on-site centers, job tenure is positively related to the use of the center. In contrast, at Central Products, job tenure is not related to use of center-based care. In general, higher education is positively related to on-site center use at both firms with on-site centers, but it is unrelated to center-based care among Central Products employees. The lack of an effect at Central is counter to results from most national studies and suggests that either the perceived differences between center-based care and other forms of care among the more educated are not as great in this area as nationally, and/or that differences by education (e.g., in income or preferences) among this group of workers are not as large as in national studies. Finally, column 4 shows directly that employees at Central Products are less likely to use center-based care even after controlling for a host of other characteristics.

DISCUSSION

Many researchers have considered patterns of child care arrangements used by parents in the United States. One of the issues of concern is to what extent the pattern we observe represents preferences and to what extent it represents constraints due to low income, high child care prices, and/or nonavailability of alternatives. These studies have not included employer-based child care arrangements explicitly. The analysis presented here indicates that a substantial number of parents will choose on-site care when it is available or will choose to be employed at a firm that has on-site child care. This may be, in part, because the on-site center is somewhat less expensive than other center-based care. However, the average weekly expenditure for the on-site centers is comparable to that for paid options in general. In addition, some of the children enrolled in the on-site centers could have been in relative care arrangements, most of which are unpaid. In the multivariate analysis, we control for the availability of a relative. Having a relative available does not affect the choices of Action Industries parents, but it does reduce the probability of on-site center care for Bell Manufacturing workers, and the probability of center-based care for Central Products employees. The location, convenience, "employer sponsorship," and reliability of the arrangement are characteristics of the on-site center valued by its users. This is in keeping with Sonenstein (1991), who found, in a study of parental attitudes toward child care, that the best predictor of a mother's satisfaction with her child care arrangement was her rating of the convenience of the hours and the location and reliability of the arrangement.

At the two firms with on-site centers, job tenure is positively related to the use of the center, whereas at Central Products, job tenure does not have a significant effect. One explanation for this finding is that workers who use the on-site center are less likely to quit or to have to leave due to attendance issues related to child care. This supports the claims of other researchers of ESCC, particularly Milkovich and Gomez (1976) and Roth and Preston (1989). It is also consistent with the qualitative evidence from these firms, in which a number of employees spoke about reductions in turnover and absenteeism as sources of value attributable to ESCC. Alternatively, some queuing may be taking place within the firm for access to the on-site center slots.

The data also provide evidence about secondary arrangements, information not typically available in child care research. Users of the on-site centers are less likely to have secondary arrangements. When secondary arrangements are employed they are almost always unpaid and with relatives. Not having to arrange two types of child care during the workweek seems to be an added value of on-site ESCC. Thus, the on-site centers appear to provide more reliable primary care, relieving parental concern about child care breakdown.

Finally, we have seen that the child's age is not a significant characteristic in the prediction of the use of center-based or on-site center care. This is true at Central Products as well, but in studies based on national samples, children's age is often a significant predictor of center care, with very young children less likely to be in center-based care. This suggests that the national results may be largely driven by institutional constraints rather than by parental preferences, or that the on-site location and reliability overcome any parental preferences not to use center-based care for very young children.

The greater use of center care by employees who have an on-site option provides substantial evidence of the value to employees of on-site center care. In the two firms studied here, on-site center care is not merely substituting for other center care by employees with higher education. Instead, on-site center care is used by a broad range of employees, including those with infants, those with two or more pre-schoolers, and at Action those who report having relatives available to care for their children at no cost. The positive relationship between job tenure and center use is also suggestive of benefits accruing to the firm beyond the value to employees, if this relationship is a signal of reduced turnover among child care center users.

Notes

1. This analysis is also reported on in Connelly, DeGraff, and Willis (2002).
2. The national data come from the Survey of Income and Program Participation as reported in U.S. Census Bureau (2002b). Hmong are not excluded from the national data, but their proportion of the entire U.S. population is so small that their inclusion should not be an issue. National data presented are for preschool children's mothers who are employed full-time since the vast majority of the employed mothers at the three firms work full-time.
3. The remaining tables in this chapter are not limited to women employees and also use an age cut-off of under six for preschool children, as this is more appropriate for this location. Comparable statistics, which include children under age six of both male and female employees from the three firms, are quite similar to those in Table 5.1 as the workforce is overwhelmingly female (see Table 4.1).
4. As described in Chapter 4, Hmong families use a very different mix of child care arrangements than other employees. They are reluctant to use any caregiver other than a relative and most often work alternating shifts so that the child is usually

with one of his or her parents. This chapter focuses exclusively on the child care arrangements of the children of non-Hmong employees at the three firms included in our analysis.

5. In fact, Table 5.3, which we discuss more fully below, shows that more than three-quarters of the workers at the three firms combined who have young children live within 60 minutes of their parents or parents-in-law and the majority say that their parents or parents-in-law would be available to act as child care providers.

6. In the sample of Action employees, 10 employees each had one child on the list; while waiting, 3 of these children were at other centers, and 7 were in nonrelative care arrangements in the care provider's home. In the sample of Bell employees, 3 employees each had 1 child on the list; while waiting, 2 were cared for by their grandparents and one was enrolled in another day care center.

7. Alternatively, one could argue that employees looking for center care are more likely to choose Action or Bell as employers. Under this alternative explanation, preferences rather than availability determine the differences between the samples.

8. Bell Manufacturing charges non-employees $20 a week more, giving an indicator of the difference between the market rate and the employee rate.

9. Because center care is usually more expensive than other forms of care, one might ask why anyone uses center care over other care choices or any care that is not the least expensive. The answer is clearly that child care has value other than simply a parking place for children while the parents are working. Parents care about the quality of care that children receive and often see center care as more educational than other forms of care. Sonenstein (1991) found that parents also valued convenience and dependability of child care arrangements. Finally, zero-cost child care may not be free. Parents receiving "free" child care from a relative may be obligating themselves to pay back in kind. The cost of "free" child care may well be higher than the money cost of market child care.

10. None of the grandparents who are providing regular care for the children in the sample receive a money payment. A few parents report that they would expect to pay the children's grandparents for child care if that option were used. However, most of those reporting that grandparents would be available for care report that they would not expect to pay the grandparents for their time.

11. Action Industries was the first firm sampled, and we made use of knowledge gained from that experience at the other two firms. An example is the addition of questions about satisfaction with child care arrangements, which was prompted by comments made by Action workers.

12. As noted previously, both Action Industries and Bell Manufacturing centers offer modest discounts for the second child enrolled in the center, which could possibly counterbalance a weak preference for noncenter care for very young children.

13. The waiting list at both firms operates on a first-come, first-served basis. The first person on the list with a child the age of the opening is offered the slot. Employees may put their names on the list while they (or their spouse) are pregnant. New

employees with young children may put their names on the list as soon as they begin working.

14. In the Action Industries sample, 20 employees are on the waiting list. Ten employees have a child under age six and comprise the group of parents on the waiting list discussed earlier. Of the remaining 10, 6 are grandparents (not living with the children) and 4 are soon-to-be parents of a new baby. The mean job tenure of the grandparents is 9.2 years, of the parents is 2.2 years, and of the soon-to-be parents is 1.2 years.

15. This might seem obvious to some readers, but the employees without young children could have been pre-children or post-young children. While there are undoubtedly some of both, the older mean age, the large percentage in categories other than never married, and the longer job tenure of the sample without young children indicate that most of the sample is post-young children.

16. The sampling unit is the child, and in a few cases more than one child from a family is included as a separate observation. In theory, this can lead to correlation among the error terms across observations, which can result in biased estimates. However, the number of such cases is small enough that this would not have an appreciable effect on the results.

17. The omitted category at Action Industries and Bell Manufacturing for the type of worker also includes the on-site child care center workers.

18. The number of African Americans at Action Industries was too small to include an indicator of race in the Action model.

19. At Action Industries, all employees work flextime so that the traditional concept of shifts is less relevant. We have coded a broad band of morning start hours as first-shift workers for this firm.

20. We do not have data on individual or family income. It became clear early in our work that this question is too sensitive to ask of many of the workers, and the group dynamics of surveying on site required that we drop the question rather than ask it but offer the option of not answering.

21. Although we have controlled for having a relative available for child care, other relatives and one's spouse serve as backup providers when the child is sick or when the primary arrangement fails. Thus, we might still expect some residual effect of marital status on choice of child care mode to come from the presence of a spouse and spouse's family, even having controlled for availability of relatives for regular care.

22. For a discussion of the full set of multivariate results, see Connelly, DeGraff, and Willis (2002).

23. It is also possible that at least part of this effect is spurious in that some factors that lead to a longer job tenure, such as being responsible, are also likely to cause a parent to prioritize reliable child care.

24. The number of college graduates in the Central Products sample is much too small to allow us to use thresholds.

25. Because the positive effect of job tenure at Action Industries and Bell Manufacturing is likely to reflect, in part, reduced turnover, we were concerned about

introducing endogeneity bias by including this explanatory variable. The samples are too small to address this issue using statistical techniques, however, we reestimated each model omitting the job tenure variable in order to check for sensitivity of the other results. The estimates for Action Industries and Central Products are quite robust to this change in specification, with the results for Bell Manufacturing less so. This is not surprising given the even smaller sample size at Bell.

26. The national statistics on child care arrangements by subsidy recipiency discussed in Chapter 2 also show a bias in favor of center care for subsidy recipients.

27. When entered as thresholds as for Action Industries, it is those employees who did not complete high school who are significantly less likely to use center-based arrangements in the combined sample.

6
A Direct Method for Valuing Employee Benefits from ESCC Using a Contingent Valuation Approach

We now turn to a more direct method for determining the value to employees of employer-sponsored on-site child care to complement the indirect analysis of the previous chapter. This chapter presents a summary of the contingent valuation method (CVM) used to derive estimates of the value of ESCC to employees. We first discuss the theory underlying CVM and why it is a useful tool in the context of evaluating ESCC. We then briefly outline the empirical application of CVM to the case of employer-sponsored on-site child care. These two sections provide sufficient information for understanding the analysis presented in Chapter 7. For readers with particular interest in the methodology, we then present a more detailed discussion of issues in the CVM literature and the implications thereof for elements such as survey design and question format in the context of this case study. Other readers may find it preferable to go directly to the results of the contingent valuation analysis presented in Chapter 7.

THE THEORY OF CONTINGENT VALUATION

In order to measure the value of ESCC empirically, one could potentially estimate a hedonic wage model for a cross section of workers in which the presence of an ESCC is included as an explanatory variable for wages, in addition to standard human capital measures and other individual characteristics. The coefficient on this variable would measure the compensating wage differential (or value) attributable to on-site child care. However, this approach is not appropriate for our purposes due to a number of reasons. First, the model is based on the assumption of the existence of compensating wage differentials, which, as argued in Chapter 3, may not be valid. In contrast, CVM is not dependent on this assumption. Second, the empirical application of hedonic wage models has often resulted in nonrobust estimates. Third, the attributes of ESCC programs vary dramatically across employers; thus, the ESCC variable in a hedonic wage model is not a comparable attribute across individuals. This problem is avoided in our study because respondents are employed at the same firm. Finally, given the small percentage of employers who provide on-site child care, the sample size required in a representative cross section to obtain enough information for reasonably efficient estimates would be financially prohibitive. This problem is, in fact, why we know so little about ESCC.

Instead, we propose to estimate the value of employer-sponsored on-site child care to the employee using the contingent valuation approach. CVM has its origins in welfare economics and has most often been used in environmental economics.[1] Here, the concept of compensating or equivalent surplus was developed to represent the amount of money necessary to equate an individual's indirect utility across two states, one with more of some commodity or benefit and one with less. When the commodity in question is a typical private good, traded in a market, one can derive an estimate of this monetary valuation by observing purchasing behavior and prices. However, if the commodity is a public good for which purchasing behavior with prices cannot be observed, it is not possible to derive such estimates. Contingent valuation is a technique that allows the derivation of this money value in the absence of standard market-generated information. Herein lies its appeal within the context of environmental economics and, more generally, in the area of welfare economics.[2] Indeed, as Sen has noted, ". . . once we give up the assumption that observing choices is the only source of data on welfare, a whole new world opens up, liberating us from the informational shackles of the traditional approach" (Sen 1977, pp. 339–340).

A child care benefit offered as part of one's employment compensation package is clearly not a pure public good (i.e., there is usually some rationing with not enough slots for all employee children, and there is always some user payment). However, neither is it a pure private good. We cannot simply observe the market price and corresponding consumption levels of an ESCC. While we can observe a market price for center-based care offered outside the firm, the results presented in Chapter 5 show that parents respond quite differently in their choice of type of child care arrangement depending on the availability of on-site child care. Instead, the child care benefit must be viewed as collectively provided, not traded within a typical market context, not paid for in full at an observed price, and competing in the consumer's utility function with nonmarket substitutes such as care by relatives. These characteristics render it highly suitable for analysis using contingent valuation.

EMPIRICAL APPLICATION OF CVM
TO ESCC: AN OVERVIEW

The empirical application of CVM involves eliciting, through some sort of survey instrument, individuals' responses to direct questions about their monetary valuation of a particular good. Examples of CVM questions include, "How much would you be willing to pay to eliminate groundwater contamination in your area?" or "Would you allow the placement of a toxic waste dump in your neighborhood in return for a payment of $500 in compensation?" The former is an example of an open-ended (no dollar amount specified), "willingness to pay" CVM question. The latter is an example of a closed-ended, "willingness to accept" question, in which the respondent simply replies yes or no.

In our analysis, we use a closed-ended, "willingness to pay" question, in which the outcome of the vote hypothetically applies to all employees (referendum format). We also remind respondents of their budget constraint and of potential substitute goods, as recommended in the CVM literature, to encourage them when formulating their response to take these into account as if in a real market setting (Arrow et al. 1993; Loomis, Gonzalez-Caban, and Gregory 1994). The full text of our question appears in Appendix A with the firm-specific language eliminated for confidentiality reasons. The focus of the question is as follows: "Would you VOTE YES to a payroll deduction of $__ per two-week pay period in order to keep the child care center open?" The amount of money that would be hypothetically collected in the form of a payroll deduction was varied systematically by the researchers across respondents, thereby creating the needed variation in "price." Information on the distribution of prices used is provided in Table 7.1. The valuation information thus derived is then used as an explanatory variable in the estimation of a dichotomous choice, probit model of the decision to accept the offered child care benefit. Other covariates in this multivariate analysis include basic socioeconomic and demographic characteristics of the respondent and a control for the order in which the CV question was asked in the survey. The specification of the probit model is discussed in full in Chapter 7.

After the parameters of the probit model have been estimated, we calculate the price elasticity of the child care benefit.[3] Because the probit model is nonlinear, we must choose a point at which to calculate the elasticity. We have chosen several points that correspond to the different populations in which we are interested: all workers, newly hired workers, workers with young children, and workers with children already enrolled in the on-site center (for the two firms that had on-site centers at the time of the survey). In addition, we solve for the value of willingness to pay (WTP) for each respondent. The WTP is the amount which leads to an estimated probability of voting yes (and of voting no) of 50 percent, thus indicating indifference between the benefit and the payment offer. This is the estimate of the value of the child care benefit to the respondent. After calculating the value of the child care benefit for each respondent, we compare the average valuation of the benefit across groups of workers in each of the three firms. The value of the child care benefit to workers not using the ESCC, or to workers without young children, provides estimates of two alternative concepts of the "non-use" or existence value of the benefit, or of the indirect value of working at a firm where fellow employees have access to ESCC.[4] The value to workers with young children can be considered the sum of the direct use value and the "non-use" value. The value of the benefit to recent hires can be thought of as the value to the marginal worker. We also compare the valuation across the two firms that currently have ESCCs and the one that does not have an ESCC. The results of these comparisons are reported in Chapter 7.

A DETAILED LOOK AT THE APPLICATION
OF CVM TO ESCC[5]

While contingent valuation certainly has its critics, it is generally considered a useful tool that can be quite powerful if applied within the appropriate context and if the survey instrument is well designed.[6] Because of the increased use of the technique in legal cases that potentially involved substantial monetary compensation based on estimates of the value of environmental amenities (such as the Exxon Valdez oil spill), the National Oceanic and Atmospheric Agency of the federal government established a panel of experts to review the technique in the early 1990s. The results of the review are summarized in Arrow et al. (1993). That study and several others provide useful insights on how to construct a CVM survey in order to reduce various forms of potential bias to which CVM is subject. One such bias, referred to as hypothetical bias, may arise precisely because of the conjectural nature of CVM questions. The more abstract and less familiar the good being valued and/or the nature of the question asked, the more likely it is to obtain meaningless and, perhaps, biased responses. The application of CVM to ESCC is less likely to be subject to this form of bias than are many other scenarios in which CVM is commonly applied. The good in question in our research, a form of child care, is familiar to almost all respondents and may have already been considered by the individual within a market context (given that private markets for child care do exist). In addition, because the data collection is on-site, respondents in the firms that already have an ESCC are familiar with the specifics of the child care being valued.

In order to further reduce the possibility of hypothetical bias, we have employed a closed-ended CVM question. Closed-ended valuation elicitation techniques are generally viewed as being less susceptible to hypothetical bias than are open-ended questions because they create a scenario that is more similar to a real market setting (Arrow et al. 1993; Kealy and Turner 1993; Freeman 1993).[7] In a closed-ended question, respondents are asked to choose between the good, in our case, the ESCC, or a monetary payment. To further reduce bias, the hypothetical payment should be clearly explained, and the compensation mechanism should be familiar to respondents. We offer a payroll deduction of a specified amount per pay period as most employees are used to thinking of compensation in terms of the pay period, and, in fact, other benefits such as health insurance are co-paid through the use of payroll deductions.

Two other forms of bias often discussed in the CVM literature are strategic bias and starting point bias. Strategic bias arises if respondents believe it is in their interest to misrepresent their true valuation of the good. This would occur if they think their answers will influence either the provision of the good or their own financial situation, and that a more favorable result will be achieved through misrepresentation. Although we cannot guarantee against strategic behavior on the part of the employees, we explained to the respondents that while their answers will be useful to the analysis of ESCCs in general, and may be used to inform policy discussion on this topic (so that there would be an incentive to respond thoughtfully), their responses would not affect the provision of child care or their compensation in their current employment.[8] Closed-ended questions that allow only one opportunity to respond provide less opportunity for strategic behavior than iterative bidding techniques, in which a series of options is offered until the respondents will go no higher or lower in their valuation, or to payment card techniques, in which a menu of dollar valuations from which to choose is presented to the respondents. Furthermore, from among the alternative closed-ended CVM elicitation techniques, we chose to use a referendum-style question format. This format is generally regarded as being less prone to strategic bias than are other closed-ended formats because it introduces majority voting to require all to pay for the proposed change (Arrow et al. 1993; Freeman 1993; Mitchell and Carson 1989). A referendum question presents the respondent with a choice between an increase (or decrease) in the benefit and a specified dollar amount, with the majority response or "vote" hypothetically being applied to all voters (employees).

Referendum-style dichotomous choice methods such as the questions used here are also considered less subject to starting point bias (or anchoring) than are iterative bidding or payment card techniques (Arrow et al. 1993; Freeman 1993; Mitchell and Carson 1989). As the term suggests, starting point bias arises when responses are influenced by the values presented. Both of these alternatives to the referendum are subject to the problem that the final result is sensitive to the bid structure—to the initial bid in the first case, and to the distribution of bids in the second. For example, for an iterative bidding technique to be free of starting point bias, it should yield the same final results regardless of the initial bid offered. This has been shown not to be the case in a number of studies.

A final issue in the CVM literature relevant to our research concerns the difference between a "willingness to pay" (WTP) measure and a "willingness to accept" (WTA) measure. The following parallel examples clarify the conceptual difference between the two. For WTP, the wording is "Would you be willing to pay $X to prevent . . . (something undesirable)?" or "Would you be willing to pay $X to get . . . (something desirable)?" For WTA, the wording is "Would you allow . . . (something undesirable) to occur in return for compensation of $X?" or "would you be willing to forgo . . . (something desirable) in return for compensation of $X?" Although, theoretically, the difference between the two (which arises through income and substitution effects) should typically be small, empirical comparisons often indicate otherwise. The evidence suggests that WTA measures are more likely to be overestimated (biased upwards) than are WTP measures, perhaps because respondents are more comfortable with the concept of paying for something for which they receive utility and are, thus, more accurate in their responses. Therefore, a WTP measure is used in the majority of CVM studies (Arrow et al. 1993; Mitchell and Carson 1989).

RECENT DEVELOPMENTS IN THE CONTINGENT VALUATION LITERATURE[9]

Finally, we discuss issues that have come to the forefront of the CVM literature during the time since our survey was developed and implemented, with the objective of assessing our research design in light of more recent analysis of CVM.

Since the development of the survey instrument used here, the CVM literature has focused considerable attention on the empirical reality that dichotomous choice CVM (such as the referendum question) often yields higher estimates of WTP than do open-ended CV questions.[10] There is not a consensus in this literature as to whether the alternative approaches yield statistically significant differences in estimates and, if so, which approach is less subject to bias. The discussion focuses largely on the estimation of the non-use value of environmental amenities and repeatedly raises three concerns about the dichotomous choice method within this context: "yea-saying" or the "warm glow" effect, the "protest no," and the embedding or scope effect.

The first of these, "yea-saying," arises, it is argued, because the respondent wants to be cooperative or "do the right thing," or simply wants to expedite the interview. Because the payment is hypothetical, the respondent may simply say yes even if that is not a true reflection of preferences. Such distorting forces, it is argued, may be more likely to occur in the dichotomous choice scenario. This potential biasing effect is argued by Kanninen (1995) to be greater for bids in the upper tail of the true WTP distribution. Accordingly, she recommends incorporating into the bid structure only a relatively small number of high-bid offers. For this reason, as well as to obtain better information more generally, when using a closed-ended elicitation technique it is important to conduct preliminary fieldwork to get some sense of the underlying value distribution (Elnagheeb and Jordan 1995). In our case, preliminary focus group discussions and interviews were conducted in each of the three firms, and the bid structure used is concentrated in the lower and middle ranges of values suggested by the pre-testing.

The problem of the protest no is in some sense the opposite of yea-saying. It is typically the case for CV questions in environmental and natural resource studies that the payment vehicle mechanism is presented as, or interpreted to be, an increase in government taxation. It is argued that respondents may vote no because of an objection to government taxation that is entirely unrelated to the value of the good in question. If so, in contrast to yea-saying effects, this would result in a negative bias in estimates of WTP. While it is becoming increasingly common to follow no responses with a question intended to ascertain whether the vote is a protest no, there is not a consensus as to whether such responses should be excluded from statistical analysis (Bennett, Morrison, and Blamey 1998; Boyle et al. 1996; Haab 1999; Jorgensen et al. 1999; Morrisson, Blamey, and Bennett 2000; Olsen 1997; Ready, Buzby, and Hu 1996). This issue is of less concern to our analysis because the payment technique is not in the form of a tax.

The embedding or scope issue pertains to whether respondents adjust their valuations in a rational way when the scope of the benefit or commodity in question changes. For example, do responses vary in the expected way between a small benefit (e.g., cleaning up one section of a polluted water system) that is embedded within a larger one (cleaning up the entire water system)? This issue had begun to receive attention prior to the development of our survey instrument (see, for example, Harrison 1992 and Kahneman and Knetsch 1992), but has become a central focus of debate in recent years. Again, the evidence suggests that lack of a scope effect may be more of a problem for dichotomous choice CV questions than for open-ended CV questions. While some authors are skeptical of CVM because of this empirical phenomenon, others argue that an absence of observed scope effects may be consistent with economic theory in some cases and may result from lack of clarity in defining the scope of the benefits being valued in others rather than being a weakness of the methodology itself (Harrison 1992; Smith 1996; Whitehead, Haab, and Huang 1998). Scope effects may be less problematic in our situation because the benefit under consideration was very clearly defined and is more likely to be viewed as a distinct entity rather than as a part of a larger benefit.

These concerns about the dichotomous choice CV elicitation technique, along with its potential statistical inefficiency relative to other approaches because of the limited information collected, must be weighed against its advantages and the problems associated with the alternatives. Our preliminary fieldwork suggested that the greater simplicity and concreteness of a dichotomous, closed-ended elicitation technique would yield more reliable information than would an open-ended design or a more complex closed-ended design (Burton 2000; Cameron and Huppert 1991; Herriges and Shogren 1996; Johannesson et al. 1999; Scarpa and Bateman 2000; Swallow, Opaluch, and Weaver 2001). Thus, this was the strategy adopted at the outset of the study. Given the numerous alternative CV elicitation techniques, and the ongoing analysis of their pros and cons as touched upon in this review, one can always question such decisions. The good news is that the results presented in the next chapter are, we believe, encouraging as to the value of the approach for this type of application.

Notes

1. See, for example, Arrow et al. (1993), Bishop and Heberlein (1979), Freeman (1993), Herriges and Kling (1999), Mitchell and Carson (1989), O'Connor and Spash (1999), and Portney (1994) for more detailed discussion of the economic theory underlying CVM.
2. See Cavalluzzo (1991) and Gerking, de Haan, and Schulze (1988) for examples of CVM applied to labor market issues.
3. The price elasticity of the child care benefit is a measure of the sensitivity of the respondents' "votes" on the contingent valuation question regarding the continuation (or establishment) of the on-site child care center to an increase in the amount the respondent is asked to pay. The method for calculating the price elasticity is described in Chapter 7.
4. In environmental applications, the non-use value of a wilderness area, for example, would be the utility value the taxpayer gets from simply knowing that the wilderness area exists. Here non-users may receive that type of utility enhancement or they may benefit indirectly from the decreased absenteeism or higher productivity of their fellow employees.
5. This section can be skipped without loss of continuity.
6. In particular, see Hausman (1993) or Diamond and Hausman (1994) for a critical perspective on contingent valuation. Also see Hanemann (1994) for a review and rebuttal of criticisms of the technique.
7. Americans are typically not very experienced at offering bids for the goods they purchase, unlike residents of some countries where prices for many goods are routinely negotiated.
8. A recent paper by Carson, Groves, and Machina (1999) suggests that CV questions are less likely to be subject to hypothetical bias and, thus, more likely to elicit meaningful results if the outcome of the vote has a real and direct impact on the respondent. This is in contrast to the conventional wisdom in the CV literature that such a scenario would be prone to strategic bias.
9. This section can be skipped without loss of continuity.
10. See, for example, Bennett, Morrison, and Blamey (1998); Bjornstad, Cummings, and Osborne (1997); Blumenschein et al. (1998 and 2001); Boyle et al. (1996); Carlsson and Martinsson (2001); Cummings et al. (1997); Frykblom and Shogren (2000); Halvorsen and Soelensminde (1998); Herriges and Shogren 1996); Holmes and Kramer (1995); Kanninen (1995); Loomis, Traynor, and Brown (1999); O'Connor, Johannesson, and Johansson (1999); Ready, Buzby, and Hu (1996); Smith (1996); Smith and Osborne (1996); Svedsater (2000); Taylor et al. (2001); and Whitehead, Haab, and Huang (1998).

7
Employee Valuation
of Employer-Sponsored
On-Site Child Care

I was told yesterday that they [one of the firm's competitors] called up one of our programmers, probably our best programmer, who has two children in the child care center and said, "We would like to hire you," and she said (well, the way she relayed the story was she said), "Well, do you have day care?" Of course, she knew they didn't, but it was her way of saying she would never leave Action because of the day care issue.

—Action owner talking about the value of the on-site child care center to his employees

This chapter presents the results of the contingent valuation analysis of the employees of the three manufacturing firms in our study.[1] We argued in Chapter 6 that CVM is an appropriate strategy to employ in order to derive a direct measure of the value of the ESCC benefit to employees. Our analysis of the closed-ended referendum style CV question allows us to estimate a willingness to pay (WTP) for the benefit for each employee interviewed. We then consider the average WTP values for meaningful groups of employees and calculate the total benefit to the employer based on employee WTP. The results presented in this chapter support the usefulness of CV models in estimating the value of the ESCC benefit to employees. For each firm, the price variable in the multivariate CV model is significantly negative, indicating that employees could answer CV questions consistently and rationally. The results also support our hypothesis, based on the framework for understanding the value of employee benefits to the firm presented in Chapter 3, that newly hired workers would value the ESCC more highly than longer-term workers. In fact, non-Hmong new hires value the ESCC at more than $14 per two-week pay period at Action Industries and Central Products, and at more than $12 at Bell Manufacturing, compared with values of $5 or less for longer-term workers.

Beyond the value new hires place on the benefit as indicated by the CV estimates, we find a substantial value of ESCC to employees who do not currently have young children, with little evidence of resentment from workers not presently enrolling children in the on-site center. Employees not directly benefitting from the on-site center may get indirect benefits because they care about their co-workers, or they may gain from the increased productivity of their co-workers or from the economic health of the company in general. Regardless of the reason, the company can offer lower monetary wage payments if its employees value the ESCC. If one takes the value to new hires as an estimate of cost savings to the firm in terms of wage increases avoided, as shown later in this chapter, the firms are saving between about one-half and twice the cost of their reported subsidy to the on-site center. In addition, recall that this estimate does not include the other expected cost savings to the firm of on-site child care arising from reduced turnover and absenteeism and increased worker productivity.

The next section describes the CV data and the estimation procedure, with a brief summary of the overall model results. We then focus special attention on the price variable, analyzing the results of the multivariate estimation to understand the determinants of WTP. Finally, the WTP estimates are used to calculate the potential value to the firm of the on-site center. Throughout the chapter, the statistical analysis is supplemented with qualitative responses from the employees about the value received from ESCC that deepen our understanding of the thinking behind the votes.

THE CONTINGENT VALUATION VOTES AND MULTIVARIATE RESULTS

> *Children are the future.*
> —A 33-year-old never-married male material handler with no children employed by Bell Manufacturing explaining why he voted yes to pay to maintain the on-site center

> *I took care of my kids.*
> —A 50-year-old woman finisher at Bell Manufacturing explaining why she voted no

CVM, as described in the preceding chapter, was applied to each of the three study sites, with slight differences in the CV questions for the two firms with an on-site center versus the one without a center (see Appendix A). Unlike the analysis in Chapter 5 that focuses on the use of ESCC and, thus, must exclude the Hmong employees, this analysis includes the Hmong. Before discussing the results of the multivariate analysis and the estimates of WTP, we first briefly consider the CV bid responses themselves. Table 7.1 summarizes the bid ("price") distribution for each firm and bid response according to category. Two points to note are the relatively wide range of the bid structure and the decreasing percentage of yes responses as the bid value increases. The wide range of the bid structure is a product of the survey design and our pre-testing, and it is important for creating the needed variation for multivariate analysis. The aggregate response pattern is important because it is consistent with price theory and rational consumer behavior, providing evidence in support of the CV approach and the validity of this set of data. It is also interesting to note that the overall percentage of yes votes for Central Products, the firm without an on-site child care center, is similar in magnitude to that for Action Industries. Bell Manufacturing employees voted yes somewhat more frequently, which is consistent with the fact that the bid distribution at Bell is more highly concentrated at the lower end of the price distribution.

Using the employees' responses to "Would you vote for . . .?" as the dependent variable and the price read by the interviewer as one of a set of independent variables, we estimate a multivariate probit equation for each firm separately. Descriptive statistics for the dependent variable and the explanatory variables are provided in Table 7.2. The probit results are shown in Table 7.3. The results in Table 7.3 indicate that the "price" of the benefit consistently has a significant negative effect on the probability that the employee votes yes. Recall that voting yes is voting to pay an amount per pay period to have an on-site center. The price elasticities across the three firms are reported in Table 7.4 and show a limited sensitivity of voting probabilities to the price. Statistical tests for differences across firms find that Action employees have a lower mean price elasticity (in absolute value) than either Bell or Central employees, indicating that the responses at Action are less strongly influenced by the price offered. The difference between the average

Table 7.1 Distribution of CV Bids Offered to Employees for Payment for On-Site Child Care, and Percent Agreeing to Pay[a]

Bid statistics	Action Industries			Bell Manufacturing			Central Products		
Mean	$14.27			$11.03			$13.46		
Standard deviation	$14.48			$10.96			$11.32		
Minimum	$2.00			$2.00			$2.00		
Maximum	$60.00			$60.00			$60.00		
Bid distribution	No. of employees	% of total	% responding yes	No. of employees	% of total	% responding yes	No. of employees	% of total	% responding yes
$1–10	197	61.76	49.24	152	72.38	57.24	258	64.02	45.74
$11–20	62	19.44	43.55	31	14.76	29.03	81	20.10	40.74
$20 +	60	18.81	21.67	27	12.86	18.52	64	15.88	23.44
Total[a]	319	100.00	42.99	210	100.00	48.36	403	100.00	40.99

NOTE: The sample sizes vary slightly across tables in this chapter due to missing data for the selected variables.

[a] The CV bid offers are used in the following question at Action and Bell (the wording is slightly different at Central), with employees responding yes or no: "Would you VOTE YES to a payroll deduction of $__ per two-week pay period in order to keep the child care center open?"

Table 7.2 Characteristics of Sample Employees in the Three Firms

	Action Industries	Bell Manufacturing	Central Products
% voting yes	42.4	49.2	40.5
Mean number of children under age 6	0.45	0.29	0.40
% with children under age 6 and who also have relatives in the area	12.5	11.6	15.0
Mean number of children aged 6 to 18	0.65	0.52	0.62
Mean hours worked per week	40.5	45.4	41.7
College graduate (%)	7.1	3.5	2.0
Category of worker:			
% hourly office workers or salaried	27.2	22.6	17.0
% hourly production workers	32.4	37.2	37.2
% pieceworkers	40.4	40.2	45.8
% 1st shift	67.6	84.4	59.5
Marital status:			
% married, widowed	69.3	62.8	62.4
% divorced	14.7	16.6	18.3
% never married	16.0	20.6	19.3
Mean age (years)	35.7	38.1	37.0
% male	19.6	25.1	32.1
Race/ethnicity:			
% White	83.7	80.4	70.7
% Hispanic	0.0	4.5	0.0
% African American	4.5	15.1	5.9
% Hmong	9.9	0.0	21.4
% other (other Asian at Central)	1.9	0.0	2.0
Mean years with firm	5.4	7.6	5.8
Mean years lived in area as % of age	86.1	77.9	62.1
Miles from home to work	11.5	9.0	14.6
Number of employees surveyed	312	199	393

NOTE: The sample sizes vary slightly across tables in this chapter due to missing data for the selected variables.

Table 7.3 Marginal Effects on Employees' Probability of Voting Yes to Help Pay for On-Site ESCC

Explanatory variables	Action Industries	Bell Manufacturing	Central Products
CV $ offer	−0.0100***	−0.0193***	−0.0144***
	(0.0025)	(0.0048)	(0.0031)
Number of children under age 6	−0.0470	−0.0472	0.0364
	(0.0601)	(0.0891)	(0.0516)
Children under age 6 who also have relatives in the area	0.0055	−0.1938	0.0530
	(0.1187)	(0.1230)	(0.1033)
Number of children aged 6 to 18	−0.0286	−0.0445	−0.0668**
	(0.0330)	(0.0497)	(0.0282)
Hours worked per week	0.0105	−0.0100	−0.0082
	(0.0087)	(0.0092)	(0.0063)
College graduate	0.2228	0.2850	0.1745
	(0.1402)	(0.2029)	(0.2031)
Hourly production worker	−0.1350	−0.1354	0.0254
	(0.0910)	(0.1058)	(0.0807)
Pieceworker	−0.2129**	0.0004	−0.0772
	(0.0838)	(0.1059)	(0.0799)
Works 1st shift	0.0502	−0.0274	−0.0750
	(0.0743)	(0.1175)	(0.0652)
Divorced	−0.1553*	0.0811	0.0757
	(0.0833)	(0.1075)	(0.0720)
Never married	0.0172	0.0213	−0.0023
	(0.0969)	(0.1179)	(0.0816)
Age	−0.0039	−0.0006	−0.0054*
	(0.0035)	(0.0050)	(0.0028)
Male	−0.2128**	0.1073	−0.0931
	(0.0815)	(0.1116)	(0.0681)
Hispanic		0.1261	
		(0.2031)	
African American	0.1767	0.1620	−0.0795
	(0.1472)	(0.1117)	(0.1109)
Hmong	−0.0651		−0.2867***
	(0.1245)		(0.0701)
Other (other Asian at Central Products)	−0.0395		−0.0966
	(0.2278)		(0.1678)
Years with firm	−0.0151**	−0.0042	−0.0110***
	(0.0070)	(0.0051)	(0.0041)
Years lived in area as % of age	−0.0069	0.0349	−0.0369
	(0.0143)	(0.0456)	(0.0448)

Explanatory variables	Action Industries	Bell Manufacturing	Central Products
Miles from home to work	0.0045	0.0006	0.0008
	(0.0037)	(0.0055)	(0.0007)
CV question not first	–0.0986	–0.1901**	–0.1586**
	(0.0638)	(0.0764)	(0.0532)
Number of employees	312	199	393
Log likelihood	–186.03	–117.64	–224.74
Chi-squared	54.23***	40.55***	80.93***

NOTE: Standard errors are in parentheses. *Significantly different at the 0.10 level, **significantly different at the 0.05 level, ***significantly different at the 0.01 level. Blank cell = not applicable.

Table 7.4 Elasticity of a Yes Vote by Employees with Respect to the "Price" of On-Site Care

	Action Industries	Bell Manufacturing	Central Products	
All employees	–0.165	–0.246	–0.235	
Newly hired employees	–0.171 ⎤	–0.261 ⎤	–0.277 ⎤	
	⎥	⎥	⎥ ***	
Non-newly hired employees	–0.162 ⎦	–0.233 ⎦	–0.194 ⎦	
Newly hired non-Hmong employees	–0.193 ⎤	–0.261 ⎤	–0.330 ⎤	
	⎥	⎥	⎥ ***	
Non-newly hired non-Hmong employees	–0.166 ⎦	–0.233 ⎦	–0.209 ⎦	
Employees with children under age 6	–0.200 ⎤	–0.212 ⎤	–0.341 ⎤	
	⎥ **	⎥	⎥ ***	
Employees without children under age 6	–0.148 ⎦	–0.257 ⎦	–0.197 ⎦	
Employees who currently use on-site center	–0.307 ⎤	–0.211 ⎤		
	⎥ ***	⎥		
Employees with young children who currently do not use on-site center	–0.114 ⎦	–0.212 ⎦		

NOTE: The bracket indicates that a statistical test for difference was performed using a pairwise *t*-test with unequal variance. **Significantly different at the 0.05 level, ***significantly different at the 0.01 level. Blank cell = not applicable.

values for Bell and Central is not statistically significant.[2] This result is maintained if we limit our analysis to non-Hmong employees.

Of greater interest are the price elasticities for particular subsets of employees. Table 7.4 also reports a set of average elasticities calculated for different groups of employees from each firm. Looking at groups of workers within firms, there is not a significant difference in elasticities of demand between newly hired (job tenure of two years or less) and longer-term employees at Action Industries and Bell Manufacturing, but at Central Products new hires are more price elastic. This statement holds for both the entire sample of employees and the non-Hmong sample. The result may be due to the fact that the question about an on-site center is more hypothetical at Central than at Action or Bell as Central is the firm without an on-site center.

There are statistically significant differences in the elasticities of employees with and without young children at Action and Central, and between users of the on-site center and employees with young children who do not use the on-site center at Action. Employees with young children and employees whose children use the center are more elastic in their demand than are other employees. Recall that these elasticities come from the multivariate analysis, so age and education are controlled for in the calculation. Wages are not completely controlled for, but the regression does contain a variable indicating if someone is paid by the piece or hourly, or is salaried, which, in these firms, is a good proxy for variations in wages. One explanation for the smaller price elasticity among those without young children might be that a higher percentage of them simply consider on-site child care irrelevant so they vote no regardless of the price. Consequently, the elasticity is low not because they must have it, but because they always buy zero. In contrast, some of those with young children may consider it a viable option for themselves at a lower price, but not at a higher price. Thus, their demand would be more elastic. Alternatively, the difference in elasticities may be the result of some self-consciousness on the part of parents with young children regarding imposing their choices on others as costs.

While our primary interest is the effect of price, and the corresponding WTP estimates discussed in the next section, it is useful to briefly consider some of the other results of the probit models in Table 7.3.[3] Other than price, surprisingly few of the coefficients are statistically significant. For example, we expected that employees with young children would be more likely to vote yes, but the coefficients for that variable are statistically insignificant for all three firms. This is interesting because it suggests that whether or not employees have young children does not systematically affect the value they place on on-site child care. In addition, variables that are significant at one firm do not necessarily imply significance across firms.[4] One interesting finding is that at both Action Industries and Central Products, the length of time the respondent has been employed by the company is negatively correlated with a yes vote. This implies that new employees value the benefit more highly, which is in keeping with our theory of firms seeking to attract marginal labor force participants. Because we have controlled for age, this result is not merely an age effect. Also, at both Action and Central, Hmong workers are significantly less likely to vote yes (with a liberal interpretation of significance in the case of Action). We believe this result is related to the Hmong's strong cultural beliefs against non-familial child care. Not only will the individual Hmong worker not use the center, she knows that her Hmong friends and co-workers will not use it either.

DETERMINANTS OF WILLINGNESS TO PAY (WTP) FOR AN ON-SITE CENTER

Convenience of location, trust people here, inexpensive.
    —An Action Industries employee whose child was enrolled at the on-site center explaining why she voted yes

Tables 7.5 and 7.6 present two ways to compare employee valuations of the child care benefit by selected characteristics. Table 7.5 calculates the mean WTP for the on-site center. This is an amount per biweekly paycheck and is above and beyond the user fee for the center.[5] The mean values for the full samples at Action Industries and Bell Manufacturing indicate that the average WTP (in nominal terms) for an on-site center is between about $150 and $225 a year. This is a fairly substantial amount given the small proportion of employees benefiting directly from the center, but it is in keeping with the rhetoric we heard on the factory floor that Action and Bell employees believe that the

Table 7.5 Mean Willingness to Pay (Biweekly Amount) for Employer-Sponsored On-Site Child Care Center by Selected Employee Characteristics

		Action Industries	Bell Manufac-turing	Central Products
Full sample	Mean	$5.89	$8.53	$4.77
	Std. dev.	(19.88)	(19.93)	(21.34)
	n	324	204	397
Non-Hmong	Mean	$7.83	$8.53	$8.19
	Std. dev.	19.95	(19.93)	(21.34)
	n	291	204	311
		***		
Hmong	Mean	$–9.45		$–7.61
	Std. dev.	10.51		(16.21)
	n	33		86
Voted yes	Mean	$13.31	$12.46	$12.00
	Std. dev.	(19.22)	(9.19)	(13.68)
	n	134	98	159
		***	***	***
Voted no	Mean	$1.08	$4.88	$0.08
	Std. dev.	(18.10)	(26.08)	(24.04)
	n	179	103	236
With children under age 6	Mean	$5.60	$4.92	$8.63
	Std. dev.	(20.16)	(8.16)	(18.07)
	n	104	49	106
			**	**
Without children under age 6	Mean	$6.04	$9.67	$3.36
	Std. dev.	(19.79)	(22.30)	(22.28)
	n	220	155	291
On-site center user	Mean	$12.68	$5.13	
	Std. dev.	(22.45)	(9.53)	
	n	51	22	
		***		
With children under age 6, not on-site center user	Mean	$–0.52	$5.78	
	Std. dev.	(15.06)	(7.45)	
	n	57	30	

		Action Industries	Bell Manufac-turing	Central Products
With children under age 6 with relative available	Mean	$–0.87	$1.11	$11.04
	Std. dev.	(16.22)	(6.99)	(18.90)
	n	40	25	60
		***	***	
With children under age 6 without relative available	Mean	$9.64	$8.88	$5.48
	Std. dev.	(21.41)	(7.48)	(16.60)
	n	64	24	46
College graduate	Mean	$42.99	$19.32	$21.10
	Std. dev.	(16.93)	(7.87)	(10.55)
	n	24	7	8
		***	***	**
Not college graduate	Mean	$2.93	$8.14	$4.43
	Std. dev.	(16.90)	(20.12)	(21.38)
	n	300	197	389
New hire (employed two years or less)	Mean	$ 9.92	$ 12.36	$ 7.79
	Std. dev.	(10.92)	(8.86)	(26.41)
	n	106	97	197
		***	***	***
Not new hire	Mean	$ 3.94	$ 5.06	$ 1.79
	Std. dev.	(19.10)	(25.76)	(14.20)
	n	218	107	200
1st shift	Mean	$8.91	$ 7.21	$ 5.22
	Std. dev.	(21.22)	(21.19)	(14.91)
	n	220	171	236
		***	***	
Not 1st shift	Mean	$–0.49	$ 15.36	$ 4.11
	Std. dev.	(14.87)	(8.64)	(28.29)
	n	104	33	161

(continued)

Table 7.5 (continued)

		Action Industries		Bell Manufac- turing		Central Products
Hourly office worker or salaried		$23.42 (20.94) 90		$ 13.87 (9.21) 46		$ 8.18 (14.30) 67
Hourly production	***	$–1.33 (15.26) 105	***	$ 5.87 (8.32) 75	***	$ 8.15 (27.67) 147
Piece worker		$–0.46 (14.28) 129	*	$ 7.97 (29.17) 83	***	$0 .80 (16.53) 183 ***

NOTE: The total number of employees in the "voted yes" and "voted no" categories may not equal the total number of employees in the full sample because of missing data. The "on-site users" category may include some grandparents who are not included in the "with children" category. The bracket indicates that a statistical test for difference was performed using a pairwise t-test with unequal variance. *Significantly different at the 0.10 level; **significantly different at the 0.05 level; ***significantly different at the 0.01 level. Blank cell = not applicable.

child care center increased their companies' abilities to compete in a highly competitive market. For example, a 30-year-old female salaried employee at Action voted yes saying, "It is important beyond the cost, it reduces turnover, and enhances our productivity." Several other employees at Action and Bell made comments similar to this. However, lest we attribute it all to good public relations on the part of the personnel office, we find that employees at Central Products are also willing to pay, on average, about $125 a year to fund an on-site center at their plant and additionally describe benefits to ESCC beyond those to individual workers' children. A 26-year-old male shipping clerk at Central said that an on-site center would "save the company in the long run," and a 47-year-old administrator at Central voted yes saying, that it "would help with recruitment."

Treating the WTP values as sample observations, we can test for statistical differences across firms.[6] In terms of the full sample means, we find that Bell Manufacturing employees are willing to pay significantly more than either Action Industries or Central Products employees, controlling for changes in the cost of living over time. The difference between Action and Central is not statistically significant. This pattern led us to question whether the result was the effect of the strong Hmong presence at Action and Central. Rows 2 and 3 of Table 7.5 compare the WTP of the Hmong at Action and Central and the non-Hmong employees at all three firms.[7] Comparing WTP for the non-Hmong sample across the three firms, we find remarkably similar WTP (no statistically significant differences). Given that for employees at one of the firms an on-site center was pure fiction, while at the other firms it was a reality, the similarity of results is encouraging in terms of the ability of CV questions to elicit meaningful responses in hypothetical situations.

Similarly, Table 7.6 shows that at least 50 percent of employees at each of the three firms can be expected to vote yes at a price of $5 per pay period (which corresponds to $130 per year). Bell Manufacturing employees are the most likely to vote yes at a price of $5, with Action Industries and Central Products employees voting almost identically. The probability of voting yes follows similar patterns to the mean WTP. These results are in keeping with a 1996 Gallup Poll, which asked workers how they would respond if their employer asked them to contribute a percentage of their income towards an on-site center. Almost 60 percent said that they would contribute, with little difference between those with and without children. In fact, 54 percent of the childless employees in that poll said that they would contribute something (McIntyre 2000).

It is also interesting to note in Table 7.5 that the mean WTP for those who voted yes is substantially larger than for those who voted no for each of the three firms.[8] This is consistent with expectations and increases our confidence that respondents' answers to the CV questions are meaningful.

The remainder of Tables 7.5 and 7.6 highlights differences across selected groups of employees in their WTP and in their probability of voting yes. We had expected that employees with young children would have a significantly higher WTP than those without young children, but that is not the case at Action Industries or Bell Manufacturing. We believe that there are two explanations for this finding. The first is that the category of employees with young children is made up

**Table 7.6 Probability of Voting Yes to Help Pay for an Employer-
Sponsored On-Site Child Care Center at a Price of $5
Biweekly, by Selected Employee Characteristics**

	Action Industries	Bell Manufacturing	Central Products
Full sample	50.53	58.01	50.94
Non-Hmong	52.18 ⎤ ***		55.50 ⎤ ***
Hmong	35.99 ⎦		34.41 ⎦
With children under age 6	50.13 ⎤	49.75 ⎤ ***	55.35 ⎤ ***
Without children under age 6	50.72 ⎦	60.63 ⎦	49.33 ⎦
With children under age 6			
On-site center user	49.40 ⎤ ***	50.19 ⎤	
Not on-site center user	44.62 ⎦	51.33 ⎦	
Relative available	44.37 ⎤ **	42.80 ⎤ ***	58.42 ⎤
No relative available	53.73 ⎦	56.98 ⎦	51.36 ⎦
College graduate	81.53 ⎤ ***	74.35 ⎤ ***	71.63 ⎤ ***
Not college graduate	48.05 ⎦	57.43 ⎦	50.51 ⎦
New hire (employed 2 years	53.90 ⎤ **	62.82 ⎤ ***	55.89 ⎤ ***
or less)	48.89 ⎦	53.66 ⎦	46.06 ⎦
Not new hire			
1st shift	53.30 ⎤ ***	56.12 ⎤ ***	50.88 ⎤
Not 1st shift	44.66 ⎦	67.85 ⎦	51.02 ⎦
Hourly office worker or salaried	66.19 ⎤	62.28 ⎤	54.56 ⎤
Hourly production	44.02 ⎥ ***	51.51 ⎥ ***	56.56 ⎥ ***
Pieceworker	44.90 ⎦	59.87 ⎦	45.09 ⎦

NOTE: The bracket indicates that a statistical test for difference was performed using a
pairwise t-test with unequal variance except for job type, which was tested using a
one-way analysis of variance. **Significantly different at the 0.05 level; ***significantly different at the 0.01 level. Blank cell = not applicable.

of two very different groups, users of the center and non-users. Individuals may be non-users because they do not like the center, either from experience or in principle, because they have relatives who are willing to care for the child at less cost to the family, or because the employee is on the waiting list for child care center slots.[9] For example, a 27-year-old male supervisor at Bell with one young child and one "on the way" voted no, saying that "I don't like how they do children, the child care center is low quality." He and his wife had both worked at Bell and had enrolled their child in the on-site center for six months. At that point, his wife quit her job to stay home with their son. Also at Bell, one 19-year-old woman with a 3-year-old child voted no, saying, "I don't think everyone should pay. Some people are on the waiting list, so what's the point of making them pay when they can't even get their children into it [the on-site center]." She was on the waiting list herself. Any members of these groups may have reason not to ascribe much value to the center. Consistent with this explanation, employees with young children at Central Products, who have no experience with on-site child care and therefore include no workers who have chosen not to use it or who have not been able to get a slot, have a significantly larger mean WTP than do those without young children.

Center users at Action Industries and Bell Manufacturing can be expected to derive substantial benefits from the facility, although we cannot assume that the benefits are greater than the parental cost of approximately $50 per week. Indeed, Table 7.5 shows that users of the on-site center at Action have a greater mean WTP than non-users as a whole and non-users who have children under age six. At Bell, the mean WTP does not differ significantly across these three groups. Employees with children under age six at Action and Bell who report having relatives available to care for their child also reveal a much lower WTP than those without relatives available. Thus, part of the explanation of the comparison of employees with and without young children can be attributed to substantial heterogeneity in the population of employees with young children. In a tight labor market, a firm may need to reach the woman who does not have a relative willing to care for her child because the one who has such a relative is probably already employed. As one 32-year-old female employee of Action Industries who had two children enrolled at the on-site center said in explaining why she voted yes, "If I didn't have day care I couldn't work."

The second potential explanation for the lack of difference in WTP between employees with and without young children derives from comments we heard repeatedly in conjunction with our questions. Employees without young children talked about their friends and co-workers struggling with child care. For example, one non-user at Bell Manufacturing voted yes in order to "Keep it [the on-site center] open for my coworkers." Similarly, a non-user at Action voted yes saying, "The benefit is important to mothers who have no other alternatives." Because the location of decision making is the individual firm, the voting was much less abstract than it usually is in the case of CV measures of environmental amenities. In economic terminology, we might say that because the employees are friends or long-time acquaintances, they internalize some of the externalities.

Internalizing the externalities operates in the other direction as well. Users of the on-site center were sometimes reluctant to burden their co-workers with extra costs, even though they themselves received benefits from the on-site center greater than their user costs. They knew, for example, that Sheila, who worked in their unit, was barely managing as the single mother of two teenage boys, and they were reluctant to burden her with their needs. A 40-year-old male employee with two children aged 6 and 4 said he was not sure how to vote because "It would help me but would hurt others who did not have kids." Similarly, a 30-year-old female employee of Action Industries with a 4-year-old child enrolled in the on-site center voted no, saying, "It is not fair. I don't think everyone should have to pay for it." Further probing of respondents indicated that almost all employees supported the payroll deduction if it only applied to users of the center. Repeatedly, workers indicated to the interviewer that they were willing to pay (even among those without young children) but not willing to expect it of others.

Of course, not all responses were altruistic in their motivation. For example, some center users talked about the importance of the child care to themselves. A 30-year-old woman with one young child voted yes because "It is hard to find good day care." Some non-users who voted yes, such as one 21-year-old woman with no children said, "You never know. I might have a baby someday." Similarly, a 44-year-old woman pieceworker voted yes, saying, "I might use it for my grand-children." Other non-users voted no, saying, "We paid when we had children."

Some workers cited concern for the company's well-being as the reason why they voted yes. If lower absenteeism and higher productivity are correlated with the provision of on-site day care, and if all employees' jobs depend on their firm's productivity in light of the extremely competitive market in which these companies operate, then even non-users receive a "use value" from the child care benefit. Such arguments are echoed in the qualitative responses of many of the managers with whom we spoke. To illustrate, at Action Industries, a 30-year-old woman manager with children enrolled in the center voted yes, saying, "It is important beyond the cost. The center reduces turnover and increases productivity." Similarly, a 46-year-old woman manager at Central voted yes, saying, "It would be worth it to keep the workforce." While a number of managers at all three firms cited this type of reason for their vote, this rationale was not confined to managers. For example, a 26-year-old man employed in shipping at Central Products voted yes, saying, "A day care center could save the company in the long run." At Action, a 50-year-old female pieceworker voted yes, saying, "It stops absenteeism."

These quotations provide a sampling of respondents' thinking about their votes. We asked all respondents specifically why they voted the way they did, and Table 7.7 shows some of the results for that question. For example, in row 1 we see that at each firm, about 40 percent of the respondents voted no because they thought that not everyone should be forced to pay for the child care center. While this might be seen as a denial of a non-use value on the part of non-users, we are hard put to assign that meaning to the result given that 40 percent of the users of the Action Industries center and 33 percent of the users of the Bell Manufacturing center also give this reason for voting no (row 2). Instead, we would argue that these results represent evidence of workers internalizing the externalities. Similarly, row 3 shows the percentage who claim that they voted yes because they felt the benefit was important to all. Fewer of the on-site center users were willing to vote yes for this reason, although the difference is not statistically significant given the small sample of on-site users. Still, the on-site users seem to be unwilling to foist the support of the child care center on

Table 7.7 Percentage of Employees Voting Yes or No to Help Pay for an Employer-Sponsored On-Site Child Care Center, by Selected Reasons

	Action Industries	Bell Manufacturing	Central Products
% of full sample who voted no because they believed that not all employees should have to pay for the child care center	41.1 *n*=321	44.6 *n*=213	44.9 *n*=405
% of on-site center users who voted no because they believed that not all employees should have to pay for the child care center	40.4 *n*=52	33.3 *n*=24	
% of full sample who voted yes because they believed that the child care center was a benefit to all employees	14.3 *n*=321	27.2 *n*=213	22.2 *n*=405
% of on-site center users who voted yes because they believed that the child care center was a benefit to all employees	9.6 *n*=52	20.8 *n*=24	
% of sample 35 years of age or younger who voted yes because they believed that the child care center was a benefit to all employees	13.6 *n*=147	32.5 n=114	26.2 *n*=191
% of sample over age 35 who voted yes because they believed that the child care center was a benefit to all employees	14.1 *n*=185	21.6 *n*=102	19.0 *n*=216

NOTE: Blank cell = not applicable.

their fellow employees. In contrast, older employees who are much less likely to be present or future child care center users were often willing to vote yes because they felt the benefit was important to all employees. At Bell and Central the differences between the age groups were statistically significant at the 10 percent level with a two-tailed test, suggesting that the motivation to vote yes to benefit all employees was more widespread among younger workers.

Does caring behavior on the part of employees for their co-workers mean that this methodology for valuing an ESCC is flawed? We argue that it does not, because firms can reduce wage payments to workers if the employees value the ESCC regardless of the source of the valuation. Indeed, the results demonstrate that the expectation of on-site centers generating substantial value to most employees is a reasonable one. At Action Industries and Bell Manufacturing we find no evidence of substantial employee resentment of the on-site center, a concern raised by a recent popular book by Burkett (2000). Instead, we find evidence that about 50 percent of employees without young children (60 percent at Bell) would vote yes to taxing themselves $5 per pay period to support an on-site center (Table 7.6). Caring behavior may, however, bring into doubt the referendum style of asking the question under which the majority vote applies to all. In a context where survey respondents know each other fairly well, the referendum style CV question may underestimate the value of the benefit.[10] Further analysis of this issue in future research would be useful to the broader application of the CVM.

Tables 7.5 and 7.6 include selected additional comparisons relating to issues that often arise in discussions of on-site child care centers. Some studies have noted that such centers are so expensive that support and production staff cannot afford to use them unless the firm has a sliding-fee scale. This is not the case at Action Industries and Bell Manufacturing because the on-site centers could not survive with managers' children only: there are not enough managers in this production industry for that to be the case. However, hourly office staff and salaried staff at all three firms value the on-site center highly, substantially more so in most cases than do hourly production workers and piece-rate workers (Table 7.5). Consistent with this, we also see in both Tables 7.5 and 7.6 that college graduates value the on-site center much more highly than do those with less education. This suggests that on-site child care may be an attractive way to recruit and retain managers and other more highly educated workers, a point also made by several of the firms' managers with whom we spoke.

Top management at Action Industries noted that the unintended consequence of the on-site center has been increased attractiveness of administrative jobs to women with young children. Action's president said, "I think it [having a child care center] really sets the company culture." The interviewer then asked, "Does it do more than set company culture? Does it make people stay? Does it make people more productive?" Action's president responded,

> I think it helps. I think it has helped us attract more white-collar people, younger white-collar people that might not be working or just started. They also have some options about how they want to work and where they want to work. They probably want to work in our industry and for our company because they have access to the day care.

Action's owner recalled his decision to open the on-site center this way,

> I first saw it, as I said, as basically a way to attract line employees, reduce absenteeism, and reduce turnover. Those remain important benefits, although the absentee issue probably was never effectively encountered because, rightly so, the state laws don't allow day care centers to keep sick children. But the turnover rates [are affected], and more importantly probably than the turnover rates themselves, is its usefulness in attracting people. Some of the best line employees say that I want to work at Action specifically because they have a child care center and I don't want to be separated physically from our children. It's important. In addition to that though, I didn't really visualize how important a role that it would play in the company in terms of attracting management. It's probably had a more dramatic effect in attracting management in the 25 years that we have been down here.

Another concern in the literature on child care centers is the correspondence between the time of day of care and the time of day of employment. All three firms were running three shifts at the time of our interviews. Second- and third-shift workers are less likely to be able to use the on-site center to facilitate their employment and thus might be expected to value it less. This does seem to be the case at

Action Industries, but it is not the case at Bell Manufacturing, where the opposite holds, or at Central Products, where the difference by shift is not statistically significant. The analysis presented in Chapter 5 shows that users of the on-site centers at Action and Bell are predominantly, though not exclusively, first-shift workers. Thus, the sizeable valuation of the center by non-first-shift workers at Bell and the moderate valuation of a hypothetical center by such workers at Central provide further evidence of employee value beyond that accruing to parents of children enrolled in the on-site center.

WTP AS AN ESTIMATE OF THE POTENTIAL WAGE SAVINGS TO FIRMS

Based on the theoretical discussion of the firm's motivation in providing ESCC, one of the categories of greatest interest to the firm should be the valuation of the ESCC by newly hired employees. Table 7.5 shows that new hires have a substantially higher average WTP than longer-term workers. At Action Industries, newly hired workers are willing to pay an average of about $10 per pay period compared to only about $4 for employees who have been with the company for more than two years. Bell Manufacturing and Central Products also show large differentials across these employees. It is instructive to consider how this compares to the firm providing the equivalent value to new employees directly through higher wages. If a $15 wage increase per pay period would be needed to achieve a $10 increase in after-tax take-home pay (value to the worker), and if the wage increase had to be made across-the-board, an estimate of Action savings from the wage bill portion of the total benefits of having an on-site center would be about $234,000 per year.[11] This may even be a low estimate because of the presence of a substantial number of Hmong workers at Action. The mean WTP of Hmong employees is negative at both Action and Central. Because many of the new hires are Hmong, we recalculate the mean WTP of new hires at Action, excluding the Hmong, to be $14.87 per pay period. Using this number as the WTP of a new hire, we derive a wage bill savings using the same methodology of about $351,000 per year. Of course, the firm might choose instead to actively recruit Hmong workers. This strategy also involves costs, including perhaps larger premiums for health insurance, given that Hmong fertility is so high.

At the time of our visit, Central Products did seem to be actively recruiting Hmong employees, which is in keeping with the stance of its human resource manager against a child care center. If we look at the WTP at Central of non-Hmong new hires, we find it is $14.22, as compared to $7.79 for all new hires, corresponding to an estimated savings in wages (calculated as before) of about $355,000 and $195,000 per year, respectively. The mean WTP of new hires at Bell Manufacturing, where there are no Hmong workers, is $12.36. This corresponds to an estimated wage bill savings of about $145,000 per year.

If one preferred to base wage savings estimates on the average WTP for all employees instead of newly hired employees, the estimates would be $122,000 per year for Action, $177,000 per year for Bell, and $99,000 per year for Central. Even these figures are above the estimated cost of approximately $130,000 at Action and $100,000 at Bell supporting the on-site center. Recall too that the full benefit to the firm of ESCC includes reductions in turnover and recruiting costs and increases in productivity as well as wage savings. While we have no estimates of the size of the cost savings for turnover and recruiting, management at Action and Bell was convinced that these cost savings did exist. On this topic, Action's owner said,

> When we first started in child care we tried to, when we were asked to talk about it and make speeches, come up with actual cost paybacks and we found they were generally manipulative and arguable. So we sort of just got into the habit of saying, "Well, we feel it works and makes our company, our atmosphere, better." For what it costs, we seem to enjoy a better turnover rate than our competitors in the area and so we accept it. I feel there is a bottom line payback for all of this.

DISCUSSION

We believe that the results presented in this chapter support the use of CV models to estimate the value of employer-sponsored on-site child care to employees. Consistent and rational results are obtained from the employees of each medium-sized firm in that those offered higher prices were systematically less likely to vote yes, and that individuals who were using the on-site center at Action Industries had a higher WTP than other employees. Our findings provide evidence (albeit limited to three firms) that ESCC is valued by a broad spectrum of employees beyond those whose children are enrolled in the center, and beyond those in management. The results also support our hypothesis that newly hired personnel would value the ESCC more highly than longer-term workers. Non-Hmong new hires valued the ESCC at more than $12 per two-week pay period at each of the three firms, compared with values of $5 or less for longer-term workers. If one takes the value to new hires as an estimate of cost savings to the firm in terms of wage increases avoided for all employees, the firms are saving between about one-half and twice the cost of their reported annual subsidy to the on-site centers.

In addition to the value for new hires, we find a substantial value of ESCC to employees not directly benefitting from the on-site center, with little evidence of resentment from workers without young children. Caring among employees may explain part of the value that non-users of the on-site center receive and may also explain why some users were unwilling to "tax" their coworkers although they themselves received substantial benefits from the ESCC. Finally, as argued in the preceding chapter, the estimates of "non-use" value derived here are less likely to be subject to a variety of biasing effects that may arise in the estimation of the non-use value of environmental amenities. Overall, the results suggest that this methodology would be a useful tool for the analysis of employer-provided benefits more generally.

Notes

1. This analysis is also reported on in Connelly, DeGraff, and Willis (2003).
2. The elasticities were derived for each individual in the sample by calculating the percentage change in his or her probability of voting yes caused by a simulated 1 percent change in the price offered. The table reports the mean elasticity for the individuals in that sample group. The statistical tests for significance across groups were standard t-tests conducted as if the calculated individual elasticities were observed data.
3. In addition to controlling for the "price" of the on-site center and demographic characteristics of employees, we also control for when the CV child care question

was asked in the survey. We randomized the location of the CV question for on-site child care relative to the CV question(s) for other benefits because of our interest in multiple benefits and our concern that the order of the CV questions might systematically affect responses (Kartman, Stalhåmmar, and Johannesson 1996; Mitchell and Carson 1989). Our results show that asking the question second reduces the probability of the vote being yes. Perhaps the rigor of the hypothetical referendum question is annoying the second time through, and thus respondents register their annoyance by voting no more often. Alternatively, perhaps people understand the question better the second time. This result, whatever its cause, suggests that, in general, if asking multiple CV questions it is important to randomize their order and to control for ordering in modes estimation.

4. We experimented with alternative specifications of the CV probit equation with very little effect on the basic outcomes shown in Tables 7.3 and 7.4. For Bell Manufacturing and Central Products (but not for Action Industries) we have employee wage information and included wages as an additional explanatory variable. Comparison of coefficients with and without wages included shows almost no change in the price elasticity and no change in which variable are or are not significant. Because all of the respondents represented in each estimation work for the same firm, our occupation dummy variables are capturing most of the wage differentials. For Central, the wage variable itself is significantly negative. For Bell, the wage variable is not significant. We also experimented with including a control variable indicating whether the respondent is an on-site center user. As one might expect, center users are more likely to vote yes for a general payroll deduction to maintain the on-site center. The price elasticities were not much changed by the inclusion of this variable. Because this variable has the potential of introducing endogeneity bias, we calculate the WRP estimates based on the results without the center-user dummy variable.

5. For each respondent, the WTP is the price that would make the respondent equally likely to vote yes or no, based on the estimated model and the employee's characteristics.

6. By treating the WTP as sample values we are ignoring the fact that the WTP value was calculated from the estimated coefficients of the probit model. Given the complicated nonlinear calculation formula for WTP it is not possible to solve for the standard error of each WTP estimate.

7. Recall that Bell Manufacturing had no Hmong employees at the time.

8. Recall that a no vote is in response to a particular price; the model's results allow us to estimate at what lower price (if any) those who voted no would have voted yes.

9. Both Action and Bell had waiting lists at the time of our survey.

10. This relates to the discussion of the "protest nos" presented earlier. In our case, as opposed to arising out of an objection to government taxation, many no responses arose out of concern for co-workers. When such no responses are removed from the statistical analysis, the probit results regarding the significance and magnitude of the price effect are essentially unchanged. However, as expected, estimates of

the mean WTP are larger with this sample exclusion. We present the results of the full sample, both because of concern about the robustness of results when sample size is reduced, and because of the conceptual difference between the scenario encountered here and that discussed in the CV literature.

11. $15 per pay period × 600 employees × 26 pay periods = $234,000. This methodology provides an upper-bound estimate of wage bill savings because it assumes that the wage increase must be provided to all employees, not just to new hires.

8
Discussion and Policy Implications

The discussion of the last two chapters has concentrated on directly estimating the value employees receive from working for a firm that provides employer-sponsored on-site child care. Earlier we focused on usage of the on-site center as an indirect measure of value. Both the indirect method of analyzing child care use patterns and the direct method of applying contingent valuation to calculate the WTP for the benefit lead to the conclusion that employees with young children derive substantial advantages from ESCC, which go beyond simply having a slot at a day care center. The convenience and reliability of child care at one's place of employment, hours of operation that correspond to periods of work, proximity to the job so that visits during breaks are possible, and quality that is "certified" by the employer are additional benefits derived from an on-site center. Also important is the availability of center slots for infants. Parents at the two firms that provide on-site child care are as likely to use center care for infants as for older preschoolers, whereas national child care usage data consistently show that center use increases with the age of preschool children. This difference between the parents we interviewed and the national data suggests that the lower use of center care for infants may be the result of a lack of infant care slots at child care centers, or due to differences in the characteristics of infant care where it is provided.

The contingent valuation approach also provides evidence of benefits from employer-sponsored on-site child care beyond those attained by parents of young children. Indeed, our analysis yields results that counter the argument that non-users have a negative attitude towards ESCC, as implied by Burkett (2000). On the contrary, we find that users and non-users display a positive WTP to maintain the firm's on-site center at Action Industries and Bell Manufacturing or, in the case of Central Products, to open an on-site center. In fact, based on our results, almost half of employees without young children at each of the three firms would be expected to vote yes at a price of $5 per pay period ($130 per year) in support of ESCC. The existence of substantial value accruing to most employees from ESCC, along with evidence of caring of employees for one another, indicates that employers gain benefits from many employees in addition to the users when on-site child care is available. This is in keeping with Grover and Crooker's (1995) finding that family-friendly benefits increase the attachment of all employees, regardless of their use of the benefit.

The benefits of employer-sponsored on-site child care that we demonstrate through the quantitative analysis in this book are in addition to any gains the firm may derive from improvements in worker productivity, or from reductions in absenteeism, turnover, or recruitment costs. Ideally, one would study these effects directly as well, but we were unable to gain access from the firms to the necessary personnel data. In terms of productivity gains, many Action Industries and Bell Manufacturing workers, including those not using the child care facility, indicated that they felt the on-site center helped the firm maintain a competitive position in the industry. In addition, qualitative evidence from interviews with workers and supervisors ascribes some reduction in absenteeism to the regularity of center care. We also know from other studies that the breakdown of child care arrangements is a source of stress for many parents and leads to a number of lost work days per year (Floge 1985; Maume 1991; Meyers 1997). Hofferth and Collins (2000) show that one-third of all women with some child care arrangement have more than one such plan, and that 23 percent of all women with some child care arrangement terminated a child care arrangement during the year. They also find that ending a child care arrangement was weakly positively correlated with leaving a job. Whether overall turnover is reduced by the presence of an on-site center remains an important research question. The qualitative evidence from managers at Action and Bell suggests that the availability of ESCC was important to their own tenure at those firms and to the tenure of other managers. Because of the production focus of the firms we studied and its implications for the composition of employees, the child care centers at these two firms are not just an executive perk. Nonetheless, administrators with young children all used the center and mentioned how important it was to their own work/family balancing act. Employee responses to why they voted the way they did also provide evidence that employees with children in the on-site center are very loyal to the center and to the firm.

In Chapter 3, we discussed a model of employer decision making about the level and type of employee benefits to offer. That model implicitly assumes that firms have the necessary information and expertise to evaluate the expected costs and benefits of alternative packages. If firms are not providing on-site child care because of the difficulty of measuring the costs and the benefits of doing so, it is hoped that the contingent valuation approach we demonstrate will help individual firms to make the "right" choice. Appendix B contains the full questionnaire except for the CV questions used in one of the companies with an on-site center, while Appendix A contains the CV questions for firms with and without an on-site center (they differ slightly, but importantly, in their wording). The questions could be easily adapted to another firm or even to another benefit that the firm would like to assess. The only caution is that the probit analysis requires a sample size of more than 100 to produce robust results (a size of 200 to 300 is probably preferred).

Simply offering the CV approach and making clear the full set of benefits available to the firm from ESCC will not lead every employer to offer on-site child care as a benefit. As suggested by the theoretical model, for many companies, even with the proper accounting, the costs may still outweigh the benefits that accrue to the firm. However, the benefits to society as a whole may be expected to be greater than those to the individual firm. For the remainder of this chapter, we consider whether the government should play a role in the decision of firms to offer ESCC as a benefit. Of course, that question is somewhat naive given that government tax policy already affects the optimal trade-off for firms between wage compensation and benefits, and among the choice of benefits. For example, the tax-exempt status of both employer and employee contributions to health insurance makes such insurance a "good deal" for firms in that the value of the firm's money spent on the benefit is greater than the dollar expenditure. While such policies undoubtedly have a relevant impact on firm behavior, we focus here on policy that specifically targets child care. First we review current government policy on child care, and then return to the issue of the government's role vis-à-vis ESCC.

CURRENT GOVERNMENT POLICY REGARDING
CHILD CARE

There are currently four main strands of government policy related to child care: 1) policies that acknowledge that there are work-related expenses generated by child care and aim to reduce the impact of such expenses on the taxable income of those in the labor force; 2) approaches that specifically encourage low-income mothers to participate in the labor market by subsidizing the price of child care, with the aim of increasing family income and building economic independence; 3) strategies that make early childhood education of good quality available to low-income families, both for its own benefits and also, in so doing, providing child care that can serve to facilitate employment; and 4) policies that are aimed at increasing the quality of child care (or early childhood education) for all children, by setting standards such as group size, child/caregiver ratios, and minimum caregiver training requirements.[1] This last type of policy is different from the others in that it would have the effect of raising the cost of child care if the minimum standards were a binding constraint. However, if parents generally opt for standards that are higher than those imposed by the government, or if government requirements are largely unenforced, then policy that sets standards would have no effect on costs. Because these four types of policies have very different goals, it is not surprising that they often seem to be inconsistent with one another. We briefly review each of them as background for considering the role of the government in supporting employer-sponsored on-site child care.

Child Care as a Work-Related Expense

The two primary policies that are based on the concept of child care as a work-related expense each focus on one side of the employer/ employee relationship. Employers that provide child care benefits to their employees may deduct from their federal taxable income the cost of providing such benefits (Employee Benefit Research Institute 1990). To qualify for tax-free status, the program must be equally available to all employees (Internal Revenue Service 2001). In addition, in 1997 (which is the midpoint of the range of time over which our data were collected), 19 states provided tax incentives in the form of deductions and, in some cases, liberal tax credits for the employer cost of ESCC. For example, California offered a credit of 30 percent of the cost "incurred for establishing a child care program or constructing a child care facility in California for use primarily by the children of your employees or the children of your tenant's employees or both" (State of California 1998, p. 1). In addition, California offered a 30 percent credit for the ongoing costs the employer paid for employee children's care. States offering credits were not limited to the high income, traditionally more liberal, ones. Southern states, including Mississippi, Georgia, South Carolina, and Florida, also offered employer tax credits related to child care. For example, Georgia offered employers "who provide or sponsor child care for employees . . . a tax credit of up to 50 percent of the direct cost of operation to the employer" (State of Georgia 1998, p. 1).

On the employee side, workers who receive in-kind child care benefits may exclude the value of the employer-provided child care from their federal taxable income for the first $5,000 worth of those benefits. In addition, all two-earner families have been able to deduct part of their employment-related child care expenses since 1954. In 1976, the deduction was replaced with a tax credit known as the Dependent Care Tax Credit (DCTC), and the subsidy rate and maximum allowable expenses were raised. In 1983, the DCTC was added to the "short form" for filing income tax returns, making it available to many more taxpayers. The maximum size of the credit varies with adjusted gross income (AGI) from 30 percent of expenses (with a maximum of $4,800) for up to two children for a family with AGI less than $10,000, to 20 percent of expenses for families with AGI above $28,000. To be eligible, both parents, if married (or the only parent if the taxpayer is a single head of the household), must be employed, and each must have earnings greater than the child care expenditure. The federal credit is nonrefundable, meaning that if the credit is larger than the tax liability, the tax liability limits the size of the credit. If the tax liability is zero, then the household gets no benefit from the credit.

Just as some states offer tax credits on the employer side, states also offer tax credits on the employee side. These credits tend to mirror the federal DCTC in eligibility requirements and in its nonrefundable nature. Many scholars and child care advocates have criticized the DCTC as targeting middle-income families because the credit is not refundable; thus, low-income families with little or no tax liability receive little or no benefit from the tax credit. (See Robins [1990] who proposes that the credit be made refundable.) For example, the "Green Book" for 1997 reported that, in 1995, 13 percent of the benefit from the credit accrued to families with adjusted gross income of less than $20,000, 47 percent to families with AGI between $20,000 and $50,000, and about 40 percent to families with AGI greater than $50,000 (U.S. House of Representatives 1997, p. 874). However, given its origins as a tax equity measure to allow for a deduction of work-related expenses rather than with the purpose of alleviating poverty, it is not surprising that this policy is targeted at middle-class taxpayers.

Many middle-class taxpayers have another alternative for reducing the financial impact of child care expenses that are related to employment: a dependent credit flexible spending account. Like the medical care flexible spending account, employees who work for firms that offer this option can set aside pre-tax earnings to be used to pay anticipated dependent care expenses. A maximum of $5,000, but with no refunds if not fully utilized, can be placed in a dependent care spending account per year. Taxpayers with access to the dependent care spending account option (which does not have to be offered by employers) must choose between a flexible spending account or the DCTC (one cannot use both). The financially best choice will depend on the individual circumstances of the taxpayer, but, in general, flexible spending accounts are a "better deal" for higher-income households while the DCTC is better for lower-income households.

Child Care to Facilitate Employment for Low-Income Families

Beginning in the late 1980s, policymakers in Washington began to create programs aimed at moving welfare recipients with young children into the labor force. These included various plans that subsidize the cost of child care for low-income families. The Family Support Act of 1988 created two new programs, Aid to Families with Dependent Children-Child Care (AFDC-CC) and Transitional Child Care (TCC).[2] With the aim of moving families off welfare, AFDC-CC offered child care subsidies for adults receiving AFDC so that they could attend employment and training programs. TCC provided child care subsidies for up to one year after families left welfare.

With two programs aimed at AFDC recipients, policymakers worried about low-income families strategically taking up welfare to become eligible for the transitional benefits. Therefore, in 1990, two new programs, At-Risk Child Care (ARCC) and Child Care and Development Block Grant (CCDBG), were created that focused on "at risk" families, that is, families at risk of moving onto AFDC. In addition to giving child care subsidies to low-income families, the CCDBG had the goal of improving the quality of child care and providing consumer education about child care, including subsidizing resource and referral services.

While one can understand the multiplicity of programs aimed at serving different populations, the result was a bureaucratic rat's nest. As employment and welfare status changed, families would have to switch between programs, which was confusing and seemed to be fairly capricious in terms of who was eligible and who was not. The Personal Responsibility and Work Opportunity Reconciliation Act (PRWORA) of 1996 consolidated the four programs into a single child care block grant, the Child Care and Development Fund (CCDF). The primary goal of CCDF is to facilitate the transition off welfare. The other goal for the CCDBG of improving the quality and accessibility of child care remains, with a minimum of 4 percent of funds set aside for these activities.

States are encouraged to supplement federal child care dollars with their own matching funds, and they may also transfer up to 30 percent of their federal Temporary Assistance for Needy Families (TANF) funds to pay child care expenses. States are given a great deal of flexibility in determining eligibility for and regulations of the child care facilities they support. The result is less fragmentation for individual recipients as their circumstances change, but substantial variation among the 50 states in the level of support for child care for low-income families.

Improved Access to Early Childhood Education for Low-Income Families

Witte and Queralt (2002) discuss the trade-off that government-funded child care subsidies are making between facilitating employment and improving the school readiness of poor children. State subsidy programs differ substantially in their emphasis between these two policy goals. For example, Witte and Queralt argue that the Illinois program is mainly aimed at facilitating parental employment while Minnesota's program places a larger emphasis on the education of the children of the recipients.

Along with the child care subsidy programs, federally funded Head Start, which was instituted in 1965, has as its goal increasing the school readiness of children from low-income families. Head Start is, in fact, the largest federal program in terms of expenditure that is related to child care, with an allocation in 1997 of about $4 million nationally (Blau 2000). Historically, it was clearly not the goal of Head Start to facilitate employment by providing child care; Head Start programs have until recently been only part-day, and serving only children aged three to five.

In addition to Head Start, some Title 1A monies have lately been allocated for preschool programs that comply with Head Start performance standards. More generally, Title 1A is directed at educationally disadvantaged elementary and secondary school children. These programs, along with some full-time Head Start and kindergarten ones, while focusing on early child education, provide as a by-product child care that can facilitate employment for low-income mothers.

Increasing the Quality of Child Care

The federal government has chosen not to set federal standards for child care quality proxies such as caregiver training, group size, and caregiver/child ratios, leaving those regulatory duties to the states. However, some federal block grant money is earmarked for improving quality. Most states have some child care regulations in place, both related to safety and to the quality of care. Some state and federal dollars are devoted to the enforcement of these regulations, and other monies are used to help centers and family day care homes upgrade to meet state standards. Blau (2001) questions whether state regulations are, in fact, binding constraints because, on the one hand, enforcement efforts are minimal and, on the other hand, many centers choose levels above the state minimums.

If regulations are binding, they are expected to increase the price of child care that is covered by the regulations. Hotz and Kilburn (1996), using data from the National Longitudinal Survey of the High School Class of 1972, and Hofferth and Chaplin (1998), using data from the National Child Care Survey, found evidence that stricter regulations increase the price of care. Hotz and Kilburn (1996, p. 134) also found that "stricter regulations are weakly associated with reduced availability and reduced availability lowers use." Thus, they conclude that, at least in the case of requiring provider training in centers, the regulation reduces the use of centers and increases the use of home-based care (which is not regulated).

POLICY IMPLICATIONS OF THE VALUE OF ESCC TO EMPLOYEES

What does our analysis of employer-sponsored on-site child care imply about the government's role in child care policy and in ESCC more specifically? Should ESCC be in the policymakers' choice set? There are several economic reasons (as opposed to political reasons) why the government might choose to try to influence firms in terms of offering on-site child care.

- *There may be an information problem on the part of firms.* Firms may have difficulty measuring the benefit to their employees and to the firm itself of having an on-site child care center. In addition, managers may worry about the irreversibility of benefit decisions (it is far easier to give than to rescind), which leads firms to be particularly risk averse when it comes to experimenting with new benefits. Thus, a process of trial and error to arrive at the optimal level of benefits for the firm (and, particularly, the benefit of on-site child care) is unlikely to occur without either more information or a cost reduction in the benefit.

- *There may be an information problem on the part of parents.* There is an overwhelming consensus among child development researchers who study the child care alternatives in the United States that the average level of quality is low. Economists such as Walker (1991) and Mocan (2001) have argued that the prevalence of low quality derives from information asymmetries. Parents have trouble judging the quality of care, both because they do not spend enough time in child care centers and they do not necessarily know what to evaluate. Because it costs more to provide higher quality, caregivers have no incentive to do so unless they can charge higher fees. However, parents appear to be unwilling to pay for something they cannot see. Mocan (2001) likens the problem to the "market for lemons."[3] On-site ESCC is particularly well positioned to mitigate this informational asymmetry because its location renders it subject to much more frequent interaction with parents. Furthermore, its affiliation with the company name and its potential role in the recruitment and retention of employees create additional incentives for providing high-quality care.

- *There may be positive externalities in the selection of quality child care by parents.* One reason that parents may not choose high quality child care is that some of the advantages accrue to others beyond themselves. For example, we have argued throughout this volume that the benefits of on-site child care go not only to the users of the center, but to other employees and to the firm as a whole. In addition, if we think of child care as early childhood education, it is not hard to argue convincingly that, as with other aspects of education, there are "public good" and/or "merit good" aspects to child care that benefit society as a whole. With that perspective in mind, consider briefly the difference between the funding of early childhood education and higher education in the United States. In child care and early childhood education, the family on average pays 60 percent of the cost of care, the government funds 39 percent, and business and philanthropy cover 1 percent. In higher education, families on average pay 35 percent, the government pays 45 percent, and private gifts, grants, contracts and income from endowment cover 20 percent. Similarly, based on median income statistics in 1998, families are expected to spend 15 to 18 percent of their annual income on child care per year, but only 5 to 7 percent of their annual income on college per year (Mitchell, Stoney, and Dichter 2001).

- *There may be positive externalities in the provision of quality child care by employers.* Even if employers are able to overcome the informational and analytical challenges of assessing the value to the firm of on-site child care, their cost/benefit analyses are still likely to result in a suboptimal level of funding because of the external benefits to society of high quality care. Indeed, some of the qualitative responses of the employees we interviewed suggested their recognition of benefits to ESCC that extended beyond the firm to society as a whole.

- *There is the potential for cost savings in terms of other government expenditures.* Enrolling children in high-quality child care facilities today may lead to cost savings later on in the public school system. In this case, subsidizing child care could result in a net savings of government expenditure. The same argument can be made in terms of the employment-facilitating aspects of child care, potentially reducing both welfare and wage subsidies to low-income families. Implementing such an effort, in part, through government support of ESCC has the potential to be even more cost effective because of the ability of employers to carry some of the expense.

- *There are equality issues in terms of our tax code.* Children are not welcome in the modern workplace, and it is not desirable (or allowed) for parents to leave young children alone. Thus, nonparental child care is truly a work-related expense for the majority of parents, and the principle of horizontal equity would support the exclusion for tax purposes of all work-related child care costs. Under the current tax system, only $5,000 of costs per year may be excluded.

All of these reasons legitimize some role for the government in the provision of child care, and several specifically support the encouragement of employer-sponsored on-site child care. Furthermore, our analysis of both Chapters 5 and 7 shows that parents value the on-site aspect of ESCC so that encouraging employee-sponsored on-site child care centers would seem a reasonable policy prescription to address all of the concerns that have been listed. Availability of infant slots and the convenience of hours and location seem to be attributes that parents value, along with the quality of care. In addition, as shown in Chapter 7, because the firm also gains from the provision of ESCC, the amount of government funding necessary to encourage this should be less than for community-based child care.

Given the substantial values we find both to parents and to all employees, and the difficulty firms have in measuring those benefits, we believe that the current level of ESCC is suboptimal. Increasing government spending in this area should have substantial benefits given that only a marginal push is needed. Recall that the on-site child care at these firms was not provided to users for free. In fact, the weekly cost of ESCC to parents was about equal to the average cost of all paid care used by employees in the three firms, although it was somewhat less than center care from alternative providers. Thus, we conclude that it is not necessary for the government to provide free care in order to promote the use of higher-quality options, but that attributes of availability, reliability, and convenience must be linked with high-quality care and moderate prices. Promoting on-site child care through providing strong tax incentives to firms should be one of a menu of ways to accomplish that goal. Managers and human resource officers whom we interviewed revealed that they find it very difficult to ascertain the value of their own benefits packages. They also have trouble measuring the cost of turnover, much less the effect of a given benefit on turnover. The difficulty of assessing the effects of increasing the level of benefits and the political difficulty of taking away a benefit if cost savings are needed in the future lead most managers to shy away from any experimentation with benefits.

While the preceding statement is true for any changes in benefits, these for child care differ from many others provided by firms due to the small percentage of a company's workforce that is directly affected. In the firms we studied, between 27 and 35 percent of the workforce had young children. This may be greater than in many other industries because of the high representation of relatively young female production workers. While our research shows that non-users receive benefits from ESCC, there is still the problem of numbers. Small firms or even a big firm with multiple locations may find that they are not large enough to establish their own on-site center. In view of this, governments could do more to encourage a group of geographically proximate firms to operate a center nearby. Similarly, tax abatements to encourage the location of a firm in a given community could be offered with the provision that a child care facility would be constructed in the vicinity. Such policy interventions already take place in cases of real estate development tied to the construction of elementary schools and community centers.

Sometimes, zoning rules must be changed to allow child care centers to operate near homes or workplaces. This, too, is an area for government intervention. In addition, because the insurance liability of running a child care center is often cited as a concern by companies, the government could help by facilitating the creation of larger risk pools.

Where a lack of information is part of the problem, the government could fund more studies of ESCC. As we argued in the introduction to this book, nationally representative household-based studies, although useful for many other aspects of the analysis of child care in the United States, will not capture enough users of on-site child care for a research focus on ESCC. Funding a group of linked case studies on ESCC, or providing tax incentives and information for firms to undertake such research themselves, would be effective ways of convincing risk-averse human resource officers to take the plunge.

We do not believe that all (or even most) government support for child care should be aimed at on-site centers. In many cases, even when all benefits are taken into account, the costs of such centers will outweigh the benefits. In addition, community-based programs are needed for those who work far from home, who are self-employed, who work for companies not providing on-site centers, or who are not in the labor force but use center-based child care on a part-time basis. Employer-based child care may also tie workers to the firm in a negative way, reducing the possibility of upward mobility through job change. These same arguments, importantly, are often made about employer-provided health insurance. However, based on the findings of this study, we believe that encouraging employer-sponsored on-site child care is a worthwhile endeavor. Offering parents quality care that is also convenient, reliable, and affordable is likely to increase the use of high-level care. Moreover, on-site child care provides external benefits to both companies and our society, benefits for which they and we should be willing to pay.

Notes

1. There are other programs that also impact child care costs peripherally such as the child and adult care food program that provides cash subsidies for food served in day care centers and family day care homes for low-income children. This program is part of the National School Lunch Program.
2. This discussion relies heavily on Blau (2000).
3. The market for lemons refers to Akerlof's 1970 article discussing the problems of asymmetric information in the used car market.

Appendix A.1
Contingent Valuation Questions
for Action Industries
and Bell Manufacturing

Contingent Valuation Questions for On-Site Center for Action Industries and Bell Manufacturing, Which Already Had On-Site Centers

6.10C DO YOU UNDERSTAND WHAT I MEAN WHEN I SAY THAT THE NEXT FEW QUESTIONS ARE HYPOTHETICAL QUESTIONS?	__Yes __No REPEAT THE INSTRUCTIONS until they understand or indicate here ___ that you have doubts, then continue.
INTERVIEWER NOTES: USE THE WORD "PRETEND" OR "MAKE BELIEVE" IF NECESSARY. BE SURE THAT THE EMPLOYEE UNDERSTANDS THE HYPOTHETICAL NATURE OF THE QUESTION.	

6.11C Do you know that normally, the <u>costs</u> of employee benefits are partly paid for by the company and partly paid for by the worker. When the costs of benefits go up, sometimes benefits change, and sometimes the cost to the workers goes up, sometimes a little bit of both happens. Did you know this?	_Yes, I knew _ No, I didn't know _ Knew somewhat

---

6.12C Okay, now we are going to ask you about some possible imaginary changes in your benefits.
We will describe a possible change in your benefits and then we will ask you to VOTE on whether or not you want it.
The way the voting works is like this:
<u>THE MAJORITY RULES</u> --
whatever the <u>majority</u> of workers vote for is what happens for EVERYONE!

<u>IF YOU VOTE "YES"</u>--
this means everyone has to pay the NEW cost to keep a benefit like it is.

IF YOU VOTE "NO"
that means <u>the benefit</u> will change in the way that I am going to describe.

DO YOU UNDERSTAND HOW THE VOTING WORKS?

Imagine that the company needs to cut costs.

One way to cut cost is to keep the benefits the same and have <u>ALL employees pay some of the costs</u> that Action Industries currently pays.

This would be done through a payroll deduction, with <u>ALL</u> employees paying part of the costs.

So if the majority of employees **vote YES** to accept the new payroll deductions, **ALL employees will pay - whether or not they use the benefits.**

Another way to cut costs would be to eliminate the benefits.

So, if the majority vote NO, there would be no new payroll deductions and the benefits will be eliminated or changed as described in a few minutes.

6.13C

Now, here is the <u>first</u> hypothetical or imaginary situation, that I want you to vote on.

One way to cut costs would be to eliminate the child care center.

<u>OR</u> to keep the center open <u>ALL employees would pay some of the new costs</u>   __Yes
that Action currently pays.   __No

This would be done through a payroll deduction, with <u>ALL</u> employees paying part of the new cost.

Remember, if the majority of employees **vote YES** to accept the new cost as a payroll deduction, ALL employees will pay - whether or not they use the center.

In addition, users of the child care center would continue to pay their current tuition per child per week and the child care center would remain open.

If the majority <u>vote NO,</u> there would be no new payroll deduction and the child care center **would shut down.** Now here's the vote:

Would you VOTE YES to a payroll deduction of $\$$_____per two-week pay period in order to keep the child care center open?

6.14C Can you tell me briefly why you answered Yes or No?

1 ___ Yes, benefit important to all	4___No, too expensive
2 ___ Yes, worth it	5___No, don't think everyone should pay
3 ___ Yes, other	6___No, rather change some other aspect
Specify:	7___ No, other
	Specify:

Appendix A.2
Contingent Valuation Questions
for Central Products

Appendix A.2
Contingent Valuation Questions for On-Site Center
for Central Products, Which Did Not Have an On-Site Center

6.12   DO YOU UNDERSTAND WHAT I MEAN WHEN I SAY THAT
THE NEXT FEW QUESTIONS ARE HYPOTHETICAL QUESTIONS?
INTERVIEWER NOTES:
USE THE WORD "PRETEND" OR "MAKE BELIEVE" IF NECESSARY.
BE SURE THAT THE EMPLOYEE UNDERSTANDS THE
HYPOTHETICAL NATURE OF THE QUESTION.
REPEAT THE INSTRUCTIONS until they understand or
indicate here _____ that you have doubts and then continue.   ___ Yes
___ No

6.13   Do you know that normally, the <u>costs</u> of employee benefits
are partly paid for by the company
and partly paid for by the worker.

When the costs of benefits go up,
   sometimes the benefits change,   __Yes, I knew
   and sometimes the cost to the workers goes up,
   sometimes a little bit of both happens.   __No, I didn't know

Did you know this?   __Knew somewhat

6.14   Okay, now we are going to ask you about some possible imaginary changes in
your benefits.

We will describe a possible change in your benefits and then we will ask you to VOTE
on whether or not you want it.
The way the <u>voting works is like this</u>:

<u>THE MAJORITY RULES</u> —
   whatever the <u>majority</u> of workers vote for is what happens for EVERYONE!

<u>IF YOU VOTE "YES"</u>
   this means <u>everyone</u> has to pay <u>to keep a benefit that you already have or pay to</u>
   <u>get a new benefit.</u>

<u>IF YOU VOTE "NO"</u>
   that means <u>an existing benefit</u> will change in the way described or a new benefit
   will be voted down.

DO YOU UNDERSTAND HOW THE VOTING WORKS?

REPEAT THE INSTRUCTIONS until they understand or
indicate here _____ that you have doubts and then continue.   ___ Yes
                                                                    ___ No

As you know companies today need to be aware of costs and employee benefits cost money.

One way to keep costs down would be to simply not offer a particular benefit or eliminate a benefit the company currently has.

OR the company could offer a benefit but have <u>ALL employees pay a share of the costs</u>.

This would be done through a new payroll deduction, with <u>ALL</u> employees paying part of the costs.

Remember, if the majority of employees **vote YES** to accept the new payroll deductions, **ALL employees will pay - whether or not they use the benefits**.

If the majority <u>vote NO</u>, there would be no new payroll deductions and no benefit.

Before we begin, remind me:
  do you have a child or grandchild currently living with you who is
  under the age of 6?   _____ Child/grandchild under 6
                                         _____No child/grandchild under 6

6.15   Now, here is the <u>first</u> hypothetical or imaginary situation that I want you to vote on.

  Suppose that Central Products was considering having a child care center nearby for employees' children and grandchildren. One way to do this but keep costs down would be to have employees cover part of the cost.

Central would pay some of the costs, <u>ALL</u> employees would pay some of the costs, and users of the center would also pay an amount per child enrolled. The employee contribution would be through a new payroll deduction, with <u>ALL</u> employees paying part of the cost.

Remember, if the majority of employees **vote YES** to accept the new payroll deduction, Central would operate a child care center but <u>ALL</u> employees will pay - whether or not they use the center. In addition, users of the child care center would pay tuition per child per week.

If the majority <u>vote NO</u>, there would be <u>no new payroll deduction and the child care center</u> **would not be opened**.

Now here's the vote:
    Would you VOTE YES to a new payroll deduction of
    $_____ per weekly paycheck   __Yes
    in order to open a Central employees' child care center?   __No

6.16 Can you tell me briefly WHY you answered Yes or No?

___ Yes, benefit important to all	___No, too expensive
___ Yes, worth it	___No, don't think everyone should pay
___ Yes, other	___No, rather change some other aspect
Specify:	___ No, other
	Specify:

Appendix B
Bell Manufacturing Survey
Excluding CV Questions[1]

Bell Manufacturing Survey Excluding CV Questions

	CODING AREA
Thank you very much for helping.	
We are studying how worker benefits help people at work and at home.	Day: _____
The questions are easy.	
Your answers are important.	Time: _____
Everything you say is confidential.	
Bell Manufacturing will not see your responses.	Location:_____
Bell Manufacturing is not changing your benefits.	
Bell Manufacturing has unusual benefits.	
We are interested in how they might affect workers at home and at work.	
We are trying to help other companies know how to design good benefits.	
If there is any question that you don't want to answer, please just tell me and we will skip it.	
Again, my name is _____.	EMPLOYEE ID#
We want to only use <u>numbers</u> - not names - on the survey.	
Please tell me your name so I can look up the number. While I look it up, can you please write your name and number on this entry for the drawing for the $100 bill.	_____
Look up the employee name, have them sign their consent next to it, and then write down their<u> employee ID number only</u> on the survey.	
This survey was announced last week: Did you see the announcement?	
Interviewer Note: Read section headings!	__Yes
The survey has two parts.	__No
The first part asks some questions about you, your family, your job, and your background. Your answers help us understand your situation better.	
The second part asks you to vote on different benefits.	
Remember, we are not changing benefits here at Bell Manufacturing.	
We just want your opinion on what is important to you.	
And you don't have to answer any question that you don't want to.	
Let's get started.	

Section 1: First, I will ask about you and your family.

1.1   Please tell me all the people who live in your home with you, including children who are away at school for part of the year or live with you part-time.

For each of these people, please tell me how they are related to you (for example, spouse, partner, child, mother, friend, boarder, etc.), their age and sex.

Let's start with you.   *Code Birth to 11 months as 0 years.*

Relationship to YOURSELF Age (yrs)	Sex (Circle)	Lives with you: (Circle)
1. YOU	Male	All Year or Part Year
	Female	Full Time or Part Time
2.	Male	All Year or Part Year
	Female	Full Time or Part Time
3.	Male	All Year or Part Year
	Female	Full Time or Part Time
4.	Male	All Year or Part Year
	Female	Full Time or Part Time
5.	Male	All Year or Part Year
	Female	Full Time or Part Time
6.	Male	All Year or Part Year
	Female	Full Time or Part Time
7.	Male	All Year or Part Year
	Female	Full Time or Part Time
8.	Male	All Year or Part Year
	Female	Full Time or Part Time
9.	Male	All Year or Part Year
	Female	Full Time or Part Time
10.	Male	All Year or Part Year
	Female	Full Time or Part Time

1.2 Do you have any children who do NOT live with you?	— Yes __ No-SKIP to 1.4
1.3 Please tell me their ages.	Record ages:
1.4 What is your current marital status: Are you married, widowed, divorced, separated, or never married?	__Married __Widowed __Divorced __Separated __Never married=> SKIP to 1.6
1.4a How many times have you been married?	
1.5 What year did you first get married?	Record year:

1.6 Which race do you consider yourself:	
Hispanic	__Hispanic
African-American (not Hispanic)	__African-American
White (not Hispanic)	__White
Asian	__Asian
or Other (please specify)?	__Other (specify) _____
1.7 Were you born in the United States?	__Yes=>SKIP to 1.9 __No
1.8 How old were you when you came to live in the United States?	Record age:
1.9 How long have you lived in your current home?	Record years:
1.10 How many years have you lived in this area, say within a one-hour drive of Bell Manufacturing	Record years:
1.11 Did you graduate from high school?	__Yes=> SKIP to 1.14 __No
1.12 What is the highest grade you completed?	Record grade:
1.13 Do you have a GED?	__Yes __No=> SKIP to section 2
1.14 Have you attended any school beyond high school?	__Yes __No=>SKIP to Section 2
1.15 Which of the following schools have you attended: the Tech Training Center, other vocational training, some college but no degree, 2 year college degree, 4 year college degree, some graduate courses, or a graduate degree?	__Tech Training Center __Voc train __Some college __2 year deg __4 year deg __Some grad __Grad degree

Section 2-Now I am going to ask you some questions about your job here.

2.1 When were you hired by Bell Manufacturing most recently? If you have worked here more than once, give the date of your most recent hire? Please give us both the <u>month</u> and the <u>year</u>. *(Interviewer Note: If they can't remember the month, prompt for season and then guess.)*	Record month: (use number) Record year:
2.2 What is your job title:	Record title:
2.3 How many miles do you drive to work one-way?	Record no. of miles:
2.4 What county is your home located in?	Record the county:
2.5 How many hours per week do you usually work at this job?	Record hours:
2.6 How many days per week do you usually work?	Record days:
2.7 Are you permitted flexible time scheduling on your job? *Record any comments on the desire for flex time here.*	_Yes _No
2.8 What time of day do you usually begin work? *Be sure to record am or pm - also you can check if it varies a lot or some*	Record time: _____ AM PM or____Varies a lot or____Varies some
2.9 How are you paid? Hourly wage? Piece-rate? Salary?	_Hourly _Piece Rate _Salary
2.10 Do you have another job?	_Yes _Occasionally _No=> SKIP to Section 3
2.11 What do you do in your second job?	Record Position:
2.12 How many hours a week do you work your second job?	Record weekly hours:
2.13 How are you paid? Hourly wage? Piece-rate? Salary?	_Hourly _Piece Rate _Salary
2.14 If you don't mind telling, how much do you get paid in your second job? *Record with any necessary abbreviations! e.g. /Wk/, Mn/, Production average*	Record amount and interval/rate ____Amount ____Interval/rate

Section 3 3.1 Remind me, do you have children and/or grandchildren **LESS THAN 13 YEARS OLD**
LIVING WITH YOU NOW? Circle *CHILDREN* or *GRANDCHILDREN* or *BOTH*
___Yes ___No SKIP NEXT 2 PAGES TO SECTION 4

	Youngest Child	Second Youngest Child	Third Youngest Child	Fourth Youngest Child
3.2 Now I want to ask you some questions about childcare (cc) for your kids while you are at work.	___ Yes		___ No - SKIP to 3.4	
3.3 How much **Smart Start money** do you receive? RECORD AMOUNT AND INTERVAL				
Interviewer Note: Ask the next set of questions for the FOUR YOUNGEST children ONLY. *Use one column for each child, putting the youngest child on the far left.* *Record completed years only. For example, a 3 month old is age 0. A 20 month old is age 1, etc.*				
3.4 How old is this child?				
3.5 Who most often watches this child when you work on regular weekdays (M-F)? Use Childcare *CODES*				
3.6 Tell me how many miles away (one-way) this cc is from your home. Record 0 if at the same location				
3.7 Tell me how many miles away (one-way) this cc is from here. Record 0 if at the same location				
3.8 How many hours per week is this child usually with a caregiver? RECORD NUMBER OF HOURS				
3.9 How much do you pay per week for this child care for this child? RECORD DOLLAR AMOUNT				
3.10 How do you feel about this cc arrangement: 1=v.happy,2=hap,3=good,4=ok,5=unhap,6=very unhap				
3.11 Is there someone else who also watches this child while you are at work M-F? YES or NO-Skip to 3.16				

3.12 What is the 2nd childcare arrangement? *RECORD CHILDCARE CODE FROM LIST BELOW*	
3.13 How many hours per week is this child usually with this 2ND caregiver? *RECORD NO OF HOURS*	
3.14 How much do you pay per week for this 2nd childcare for this child? *RECORD AMOUNT*	
3.15 How do you feel about this cc arrangement? *1=v.happy,2=hap,3=good,4=ok,5=unhap,6=very unhap*	
3.16 Who most often watches this child on Saturday if you need to work? *Use Childcare CODES or Z*	
3.17 How do you feel about this cc arrangement? *1=v.happy,2=hap,3=good,4=ok,5=unhap,6=very unhap*	
3.18 Would you consider using A Child's View for this child on Saturdays that you need to work? *1=Yes definitely, 2=Maybe, depends on charge (price), 3=Once in a while,4=Probably Not, 5=No*	

CODES FOR CHILDCARE ARRANGEMENTS:

A - BELL'S CENTER/A CHILD'S VIEW

B - YOUR SPOUSE OR CHILD'S OTHER PARENT

C - GRANDPARENT IN YOUR HOME

D - GRANDPARENT IN THEIR HOME

E - ADULT RELATIVE IN YOUR HOME

F - ADULT RELATIVE IN THEIR HOME

G - NON-RELATIVE IN YOUR HOME

H - NON-RELATIVE IN THEIR HOME

I - AT HOME WITH OLDER CHILDREN

J - HOME ALONE

K - OTHER CENTER

L - AT SCHOOL. This is usual primary care for school age children

M - OTHER (*PLEASE SPECIFY*)_____

N - DON'T KNOW

Z - NEVER WORKS ON SATURDAY-Skip to next pg

comments here re: *CC AVAILABILITY*

Section 3 cont.

Only for people _with children or grandchildren under age 13_ living at home.	*START HERE FOR ANYONE WITHOUT CHILDREN UNDER 13!*
Now we would like to ask you some questions about other types of childcare that might be available to you. DO NOT include the child care arrangements that you are currently using in your answers.	
3.50 Do you know of any daycare center, other than Bell's, that your children could attend while you are at work?	__Yes __No=> SKIP to 3.52
3.51 How much would you expect to pay per week per child for the one you would most likely use?	Record amount:
3.52 Do you have a parent or parent-in-law, who is not currently caring for your child(ren), who does not live with you but lives within 30 minutes of you?	__Yes=>SKIP to 3.54 __No
3.53 Within 60 minutes?	__Yes __No=>SKIP to 3.56
3.54 Would any of these parents or in-laws be available to care for your children on a <u>regular</u> basis while you are at work?	__Yes __No=>SKIP to 3.56
3.55 How much would you expect to pay your parents or in-laws per week per child? (*Interviewer Note: If they would not expect to pay anything, please record 0. Record "G" if they help buy groceries, record "H" if they help around the house/yard, etc.*)	Record amount:
3.56 Do you have any other relatives, who are not currently caring for your children, who do not live with you, but live within 30 minutes of you?	__Yes=>SKIP to 3.58 __No
3.57 Within 60 minutes:	__Yes __No=>SKIP to 3.60
3.58 Would any of these relatives be available to care for your children on a <u>regular</u> basis while you are at work?	__Yes __No=>SKIP to 3.60
3.59 How much would you expect to pay these relatives per week per child? (*Interviewer Note: If they would not expect to pay anything, please record 0. Record "G" if they help buy groceries, record "H" if they help around the house/yard, etc.*)	Record amount
3.60 Do you know of anyone else who might be available to care for your children in your home or their home on a <u>regular</u> basis while you are at work:	__Yes __No=>SKIP to 3.62
3.61 How much would you expect to pay this other person per week per child? (*Interviewer Note: If they would not expect to pay anything, please record 0. Record "G" if they help buy groceries, record "H" if they help around the house/yard, etc.*)	Record amount

Section 4–Remind me, are you currently married?	__Yes __No=>SKIP to Section 5
4.1 We would like to ask some questions about your spouse. Did your spouse graduate from high school?	__Yes=>SKIP to 4.4 __No
4.2 What is the highest grade he/she completed	Record grade:
4.3 Does your spouse have a GED?	__Yes __No=>SKIP to 4.6
4.4 Has your spouse attended any school beyond high school?	__Yes __No=>SKIP to 4.6

4.5   Which of the following best describes your spouse's highest level of education:
         tech training,
         other vocational training,
         some college but no degree,
         2 year college degree,
         4 year college degree,
         some graduate courses,
         or a graduate degree?
	__Tech Training
	__Voc train
	__Some college
	__2 year deg
	__4 year deg
	__Some grad
	__Grad degree

4.6 Is your spouse currently employed?	__Yes=>SKIP to 4.8 __No

4.7   Please tell me which of the following most accurately describes your spouse's employment status. My spouse is currently:
         on lay-off
         in school
         a homemaker
         unable to work because of health problems
         not employed and looking for a job
         not employed and not looking for a job
	__Lay-off=>
	__School=>
	__Homemaker
	__Health prob=>
	__Looking for a job=>
	__Not looking for a job=>
	    SKIP to Section 5

4.8 Does your spouse have more than one job?	__Yes __No
4.9 How many hours per week does he/she usually work? (with all jobs together)?	Record hours:

4.10 Would you say that your work times are
         the same as your spouse
         nearly the same
         overlap about half the time
         very different
         completely opposite
	__the same as your spouse
	__nearly the same
	__overlap about half the time
	__very different
	__completely opposite

4.11 If you don't mind telling, what is your spouse's annual gross income from wages, salary and bonuses from all their jobs? Even a ballpark estimate is helpful to us in understanding your situation.	Record income:

Section 5. Now I am going to ask you questions about your family when you were growing up. These answers are really important to understanding your situation growing up and what you think about different benefits. We can skip anything that you don't want to answer. No problem:

5.1 In what state in the US or in what foreign country were your parents born? *(Interviewer Note: If they do not know where either parent was born, please record "Don't Know," or "US" or "foreign" if known.)*	Mother: _____ Father: _____

5.2 When you were a child did you grow up in the city, the suburbs, a small town, or in the country? *(Interviewer Note: If more than one type of place, where did they live the majority of the time or check "Moved a lot.")*	__Urban __Suburban __Town __Rural __Moved a lot

5.3 Which of the categories I am about to list comes closest to describing your living situation for most of the time as a child: lived with both own mother and father lived with own mother and stepfather lived with own father and stepmother lived with own mother only lived with own father only or other (please specify for other)? *Interviewer Note: If two situations are offered record the longest duration situation. If they are similar in length, record the more recent one.*	__Moth & fath __Moth & step-f __Fath & step-m __Mother only __Father only __Other (specify): _____

5.4 What was your religious affiliation <u>when you were a child</u>?	__No religion __Catholic __Baptist __Episcopalian __Lutheran __Methodist __Presbyterian __Mormon __United Church __Pentecostal __Jehovah's Witness __Other Prot. Fundamentalist __Other Prot. Non-Fundamentalist __Jewish __All other
5.5 How often did your family attend church services when you were <u>a child</u>?	__More than 1/wk __About 1/wk __2 or 3/month __About 1/month __Several times/ year or less __Not at all

5.6 What is your religious affiliation now?	__No religion __Catholic __Baptist __Episcopalian __Lutheran __Methodist __Presbyterian __Mormon __United Church __Pentecostal __Jehovah's Witness __Other Prot. Fundamentalist __Other Prot. Non-Fundamentalist __Jewish __All other
5.7 How often do you attend church services now?	__More than 1/wk __About 1/wk __2 or 3/month __About 1/month __Several times/ year or less __Not at all
5.8 Which of the following best describes the income of your family when you were growing up: (very low, low, average, high, very high)?	__Very low __Low __Average __High __Very High
5.9 Did your mother work before you started first grade?	__Yes __No __Don't know
5.10 Which of the following categories best describes your mother's level of education: (did not complete high school, high school but no college, some college but no degree, 2-year degree, 4-year degree, Masters of Ph.D.)?	__Less than high school __High school __Some college __2 year deg. __4 year deg. __Master/Ph.D. __Don't know

5.11 Which of the following categories best describes your father's level of education: (did not complete high school, high school but no college, some college but no degree, 2-year degree, 4-year degree, Masters of Ph.D.)?	__Less than high school __High school __Some college __2 year deg. __4 year deg. __Master/Ph.D. __Don't know
5.12 How many brothers and sisters did you have including stepbrothers, stepsisters, children adopted by your parents, and siblings who have died?	Record #:
NOW WE ARE GOING TO GO TO THE "VOTING" PART OF THE SURVEY. READY? LET'S START.	

Section 6: CV Questions—See Appendix A.1 and A.2

Section 7 – I really appreciate your time in answering these questions. We are almost finished.	
The next set of questions asks about the most recent job you held before this one and about total years of work experience.	
7.1 Have you worked at Bell Manufacturing before? *Interviewer Note: be sure that they totally left the company and then came back before you check YES. Internal job changes within the company code as NO*	__Yes __No
7.2 Have you worked at other companies before?	__Yes __No - SKIP to section 9
7.3a Was this job also in the same industry?	__Yes __No
7.3b What was your previous job title?	Record Title:
7.4 When did you start that job? Please give me both the month and the year. *(Interviewer Note: If they can't remember the month, prompt for season and then guess.)*	Record month:_____ Record year: _____
7.5 When did you leave that job?	Record month:_____ Record year: _____
7.6 While you were working at this previous job, did you have any children less than 6 years old?	__Yes __No=> SKIP to 7.8

7.7 What was the primary type of child care you used while you were at work for that job? *Interviewer Note: If they say "center care," prompt for whether it was the firm's center. Also you may have to prompt for location - "YOUR" home or "THEIR" home*	__Bell Manufacturing's center __Your spouse or child's other parent __Grandparent in YOUR home __Grandparent in THEIR home __Adult relative in YOUR home __Adult relative in THEIR home __Non-relative in YOUR home __Non-relative in THEIR home __Home w/older children __Home alone __Other center __At school __Other (specify _____) __Don't know
7.8 In what year did you first start working most of the year at a regular job?	Record year:
7.9 How many years of full-time work have you worked since that year?	Record number of years:
7.10 How many times have you stopped working for more than three months since the first year that you started working at a regular job?	Record number of times:

Section 8 – This is the last section. Thank you again for your patience.	
8.1 Does anyone in your household currently receive food stamps?	__Yes __No
8.2 Does anyone in your household currently receive a rent subsidy?	__Yes __No
8.3 Does anyone in your household currently receive AFDC?	—Yes __No
8.4 Does anyone in your household currently receive any other type of assistance?	__Yes __No=>SKIP to 8.6
8.5 What type of assistance?	Record type:
8.6 Does anyone in your household currently receive child support payments?	__Yes __No=>SKIP to 8.8
8.7 How much child support is usually received per month?	Record amount:
8.8 Does anyone in your household currently pay child support? *Record any notes about differences between what child support is awarded versus what is actually paid here.*	__Yes __No=>SKIP to 8.10
8.9 How much child support is usually paid per month?	Record amount:
8.10 Remind me, other than yourself (and your spouse), are there any people over 18 years of age who live with you?	__Yes __No=>SKIP to end
8.11 Finally, which of the following best describes how household expenses are shared with these adults other than your spouse: • all household expenses are shared • some are shared • none are shared	__All shared __Some shared __None shared

THAT'S IT! <u>Thank you very much</u> for your time and your careful answers to our questions. Your help was important! WE APPRECIATE IT A LOT!
Please tell the folks who work around you how much we need their opinions too.
Get them to sign up or let me know they are willing to help out, too.
I will be sure to put your name in the drawing for the $100 bill.
Good luck and thank you again.

Note

1. The questionnaires for Action Industries and Central Products are almost identical to those for Bell Manufacturing, differing only due to firm-specific tailoring of wording and the addition of a small number of questions following the initial interviews at Action.

References

Adolf, Barbara, and Karol Rose. 1985. *The Employer's Guide to Child Care: Developing Programs for Working Parents*. New York: Praeger.

Akerlof, George. 1970. "The Market for 'Lemons': Quality Uncertainty and the Market Mechanism." *Quarterly Journal of Economics* 84(3): 488–500.

Arrow, Kenneth, Robert Solow, Paul Portney, Edward Leamer, Roy Radner, and Howard Schuman. 1993. "Contingent Valuation Methodology Report, Report of the NOAA Panel on Contingent Valuation." *Federal Register* 58(10): 4602–4612.

Auerbach, Judith. 1990. "Employer-Supported Child Care as a Women-Responsive Policy Issue: The Impact of Workplace Family Policies." *Journal of Family Issues* 11(4): 384–400.

Bennett, Jeff, Mark Morrison, and Russell Blamey. 1998. "Testing the Validity of Responses to Contingent Valuation Questioning." *Australian Journal of Agricultural and Resource Economics* 42(2): 131–148.

Benson, Joseph, and Arthur Whatley. 1994. "Pros and Cons of Employer Sponsored Child Care." *Journal of Compensation and Benefits* 9(4): 16–20.

Bianchi, Suzanne M. 2000. "Maternal Employment and Time with Children: Dramatic Change or Surprising Opportunity?" *Demography* 37(4): 401–414.

Bishop, Richard, and Thomas Heberlein. 1979. "Measuring Values of Extra-Market Goods: Are Indirect Measures Biased?" *American Journal of Agricultural Economics* 61(5): 926–930.

Bjornstad, David, Ronald Cummings, and Laura Osborne. 1997. "A Learning Design for Reducing Hypothetical Bias in the Contingent Valuation Method." *Environmental and Resource Economics* 10(3): 207–221.

Blau, David. M. 2000. "Child Care Subsidy Programs." NBER working paper no. 7806. Washington, DC: National Bureau of Economic Research.

———— 2001. *The Child Care Problem: An Economic Analysis*. New York: Russell Sage.

Blau, David M., and Alison Hagy. 1998. "The Demand for Quality in Child Care Centers." *Journal of Political Economy* 106(1): 104–146.

Blau, David M., and Philip K. Robins. 1988. "Child-Care Costs and Family Labor Supply." *Review of Economics and Statistics* 70(3): 374–381.

Blau, Francine, Marianne Ferber, and Anne Winkler. 1998. *The Economics of Women, Men, and Work*. 3d ed. Upper Saddle River, NJ: Prentice Hall.

Blumenschein, Karen, Magnus Johannesson, Glenn C. Blomquist, Bengt Liljas, and Richard M. O'Connor. 1998. "Experimental Results on Expressed

Certainty and Hypothetical Bias in Contingent Valuation." *Southern Economic Journal* 65(1): 169–177.

Blumenschein, Karen, Magnus Johannesson, Krista K. Yokoyama, and Patricia R. Freeman. 2001. "Hypothetical versus Real Willingness to Pay in the Health Care Sector: Results from a Field Experiment." *Journal of Health Economics* 20(3): 441–457.

Boyle, Kevin J., F. Reed Johnson, Daniel W. McCollum, William H. Desvousges, Richard W. Dunford, and Sara P. Hudson. 1996. "Valuing Public Goods: Discrete versus Continuous Contingent-Valuation Responses." *Land Economics* 72(3): 381–396.

Brayfield, April, and Sandra L. Hofferth. 1995. "Balancing the Family Budget: Differences in Child Care Expenditures by Race/Ethnicity, Economic Status, and Family Structure." *Social Science Quarterly* 76(1): 158–177.

Burkett, Elinor. 2000. *The Baby Boon: How Family-Friendly America Cheats the Childless.* New York: Free Press.

Burton, Michael. 2000. "A Semi-parametric Estimator of Willingness-to-Pay Applied to Dichotomous Choice Contingent Valuation Data." *Australian Economic Papers* 39(2): 200–214.

Cameron, Trudy Ann, and Daniel D. Huppert. 1991. "Referendum Contingent Valuation Estimates: Sensitivity to the Assignment of Offered Values." *Journal of the American Statistical Association* 86(416): 910–918.

Carlsson, Frederik, and Peter Martinsson. 2001. "Do Hypothetical and Actual Marginal Willingness to Pay Differ in Choice Experiments?" *Journal of Environmental Economics and Management* 41(2): 179–192.

Carson, Richard, Theodore Groves, and Mark Machina. 1999. "Incentive and Informational Properties of Preference Questions." Plenary address, European Association of Resources and Environmental Economists, Oslo, Norway, June.

Casper, Lynne M. 1995. "What Does It Cost to Mind Our Preschoolers?" *U.S. Census Bureau Current Population Reports* P70-52. http://www.census.gov/prod/l/pop/p70-52.pdf (accessed September 10, 2003).

Cavalluzzo, Linda C. 1991. "Nonpecuniary Rewards in the Workplace: Demand Estimates Using Quasi-Market Data." *Review of Economics and Statistics* 71(3): 508–512.

Chaplin, Duncan, Philip Robins, Sandra Hofferth, Douglas Wissoker, and Paul Fronstin. 1996. "The Price Elasticity of Child Care Demand: A Sensitivity Analysis." Unpublished manuscript. Washington, DC: Urban Institute.

Connelly, Rachel, Deborah S. DeGraff, and Rachel Willis. 2002. "If You Build It, They Will Come: Parental Use of On-Site Child Care Centers." *Population Research and Policy Review* 21(3): 241–273.

———— Forthcoming. "The Value of Employer-Sponsored Child Care to Employees." *Industrial Relations: A Journal of Economy and Society.*

Connelly, Rachel, and Jean Kimmel. 2003. "Marital Status and Full-time/Part-time Work Status in Child Care Choices." *Applied Economics* 35(7): 761–777.

Creed, Michael, Christi Allen, and C. Janet Whitney. 1994. "Packaging Benefits Packages." *Journal of Management in Engineering* 10(1): 19–22.

Cummings, Ronald G., Steven Elliott, Glenn W. Harrison, and James Murphy. 1997. "Are Hypothetical Referenda Incentive Compatible?" *Journal of Political Economy* 105(3): 609–621.

Davis, Elizabeth, and Rachel Connelly. 2003. "The Influence of Local Price and Availability on Parents' Choice of Child Care." Working paper. St Paul, MN: Department of Applied Economics, University of Minnesota.

Diamond, Peter A., and Jerry A. Hausman. 1994. "Contingent Valuation: Is Some Number Better than No Number?" *Journal of Economic Perspectives* 8(4): 45–64.

Duncan, Greg, and C. Russell Hill. 1977. "The Child Care Mode Choice of Working Mothers." In *Five Thousand American Families—Patterns of Economic Progress*, Greg Duncan and James N. Morgan, eds. Ann Arbor, MI: Survey Research Center in the Institute of Social Research, University of Michigan, pp. 379–388.

Elnagheeb, Abdelmoneim H., and Jeffrey L. Jordan. 1995. "Comparing Three Approaches that Generate Bids for the Referendum Contingent Valuation Method." *Journal of Environmental Economics and Management* 29(1): 92–104.

Employee Benefit Research Institute. 1990. *Fundamentals of Employee Benefit Programs.* 4th ed. Washington, DC: Employee Benefit Research Institute.

Families and Work Institute. 1998. *Business Work-Life Study Executive Summary.* New York. http://familiesandwork.org/summary/worklife.pdf (accessed June 1, 2003).

Floge, Lillian. 1985. "The Dynamics of Child Care Use and Some Implications for Women's Employment." *Journal of Marriage and the Family* 47(1): 143–154.

Flynn, Gillian. 1995. "Deciding How to Provide Dependent Care Isn't Child's Play." *Personnel Journal* 74(10): 92.

Folk, Karen Fox, and Andrea Beller. 1993. "Part-time Work and Child Care Choices for Mothers of Preschool Children." *Journal of Marriage and the Family* 55(1): 146–157.

Freeman, A. Myrick III. 1993. *The Measurement of Environmental and Resource Values: Theory and Methods*. Washington, DC: Resources for the Future.

Friedman, Dana. 1987. "Family-Supportive Policies: The Corporate Decision-Making Process." New York: Conference Board Research Report 897.

―――. 1989. "Impact of Child Care on the Bottom Line." In *Investing in People: A Strategy to Address America's Workforce Crisis*, Vol. 2. Commission on Workforce Quality and Labor Market Efficiency. Washington, DC: U.S. Department of Labor, pp. 1427–1476.

Frykblom, Peter, and Jason F. Shogren. 2000. "An Experimental Testing of Anchoring Effects in Discrete Choice Questions." *Environmental and Resource Economics* 16(3): 329–341.

Galinsky, Ellen. 1986. "Family Life and Corporate Policies." In *In Support of Families*, Michael W. Yogman and T. Berry Brazelton, eds. Cambridge, MA: Harvard University Press, pp. 109–145; 266–272.

Gerking, Shelby, Menno de Haan, and William Schulze. 1988. "The Marginal Value of Job Safety: A Contingent Valuation Study." *Journal of Risk and Uncertainty* 1(2): 185–200.

Glass, Jennifer, and Tetsushi Fujimoto. 1995. "Employer Characteristics and the Provision of Family Responsive Policies." *Work and Occupations* 22(4): 380–411.

Goff, Stephen, Michael Mount, and Rosemary Jamison. 1990. "Employer Supported Child Care, Work/Family Conflict, and Absenteeism: A Field Study." *Personnel Psychology* 43: 793–808.

Goldberg, Wendy, Ellen Greenberger, Judith Koch-Jones, Robin O'Neil, and Sharon Hamill. 1989. "Attractiveness of Child Care and Related Employer-Supported Benefits and Policies to Married and Single Parents." *Child and Youth Care Quarterly* 18(1): 23–37.

Greenberger, Ellen, Wendy Goldberg, Sharon Hamill, Robin O'Neil, and Constance Payne. 1989. "Contributions of a Supportive Work Environment to Parent's Well-Being and Orientation to Work." *American Journal of Community Psychology* 17(6): 755–783.

Grover, Steven L., and Karen J. Crooker. 1995. "Who Appreciates Family-Responsive Human Resource Policies: The Impact of Family Friendly Policies on the Organizational Attachment of Parents and Non-Parents." *Personnel Psychology* 48(2): 271–288.

Haab, Timothy C. 1999. "Nonparticipation or Misspecification? The Impacts of Nonparticipation on Dichotomous Choice Contingent Valuation." *Environmental and Resource Economics* 14(4): 443–461.

Halvorsen, Bente, and Kjartan Soelensminde. 1998. "Differences between Willingness-to-Pay Estimates from Open-Ended and Discrete-Choice Contingent Valuation Methods: The Effects of Heteroscedasticity." *Land Economics* 74(2): 262–282.

Han, Wen-Jui. 1999. "Child Care Choices among Employed Mothers with Preschool Children." Working paper. New York: Columbia University School of Social Work.

Hanemann, Michael W. 1994. "Valuing the Environment through Contingent Valuation." *Journal of Economic Perspectives* 8(4): 19–43.

Harrison, Glenn W. 1992. "Valuing Public Goods with the Contingent Valuation Method: A Critique of Kahneman and Knetsch." *Journal of Environmental Economics and Management* 23(3): 248–257.

Hausman, Jerry, ed. 1993. *Contingent Valuation: A Critical Assessment.* New York: Elsevier Press.

Herriges, Joseph A., and Catherine L. Kling, eds. 1999. *Valuing Recreation and the Environment: Revealed Preference Methods in Theory and Practice.* Northampton, MA: Elgar Publishing.

Herriges, Joseph A., and Jason F. Shogren. 1996. "Starting Point Bias in Dichotomous Choice Valuation with Follow-Up Questioning." *Journal of Environmental Economics and Management* 30(1): 112–131.

Hofferth, Sandra, and Duncan D. Chaplin. 1998. "State Regulations and Child Care Choice." *Population Research and Policy Review* 17(2): 111–140.

Hofferth, Sandra, and Nancy Collins. 2000. "Child Care and Employment Turnover." *Population Research and Policy Review* 19(4): 357–395.

Hofferth, Sandra, and Douglas Wissoker. 1992. "Price, Quality and Income in Child Care Choices." *Journal of Human Resources* 27(1): 70–111.

Holmes, Thomas P., and Randall A. Kramer. 1995. "An Independent Sample Test of Yea-Saying and Starting Point Bias in Dichotomous-Choice Contingent Valuation." *Journal of Environmental Economics and Management* 29(1): 121–132.

Hotz, V. Joseph, and M. Rebecca Kilburn. 1992. "Estimating the Demand for Child Care and Child Care Costs: Should We Ignore Families with Non-Working Mothers?" Unpublished manuscript, UCLA, Los Angeles, CA.

———. 1996. "Regulating Child Care: The Effects of State Regulations on Child Care Demand and Its Costs." Working paper, UCLA, Los Angeles, CA.

Internal Revenue Service. 2001. "Dependent Care Assistance." *Department of Treasury: The Digital Daily.* http://www.irs.gov/formspubs/display/ 0,,i1%3D50%26genericId%3D79359,00.html (accessed June 2, 2003).

Johannesson, Magnus, Glenn C. Blomquist, Karen Blumenschein, Per-Olov Johansson, Bengt Liljas, and Richard M. O'Connor. 1999. "Calibrating Hypothetical Willingness to Pay Response." *Journal of Risk and Uncertainty* 18(1): 21–32.

Johansen, Anne, Arleen Leibowitz, and Linda Waite. 1996. "The Importance of Child-Care Characteristics to Choice of Care." *Journal of Marriage and the Family* 58(3): 759–772.

Jorgensen, Bradley S., Geoffrey J. Syme, Brian J. Bishop, and Blair E. Nancarrow. 1999. "Protest Response in Contingent Valuation." *Environmental and Resource Economics* 14(1): 131–150.

Kahneman, Daniel, and Jack L. Knetsch. 1992. "Valuing Public Goods: The Purchase of Moral Satisfaction." *Journal of Environmental Economics and Management* 22(1): 57–70.

Kanninen, Barbara J. 1995. "Bias in Discrete Response Contingent Valuation." *Journal of Environmental Economics and Management* 28(1): 114–125.

Kartman, Bernt, Nils-Olov Stalhåmmar, and Magnus Johannesson. 1996. "Valuation of Health Changes with the Contingent Valuation Method: A Test of Scope and Question Order Effects." *Health Economics* 5(6): 531–541.

Kealy, Mary Jo, and Robert W. Turner. 1993. "A Test of the Equality of Closed-Ended and Open-Ended Contingent Valuations." *American Journal of Agricultural Economics* 75(2): 321–331.

Kimmel, Jean. 1995. "The Effectiveness of Child Care Subsidies in Encouraging the Welfare to Work Transition of Low Income Single Mothers." *American Economic Review Papers and Proceedings* 85(2): 271–275.

———. 1998. "Child Care Costs as a Barrier to Employment for Single and Married Mothers." *Review of Economics and Statistics* 80(2): 287–299.

Kossek, Ellen, and Victor Nichol. 1992. "The Effects of On-Site Child Care on Employee Attitudes and Performance." *Personnel Psychology* 45(3): 485–509.

Krug, David, V. Palmour, and M. Ballassai. 1972. *Evaluation of the Office of Economic Opportunity Child Development Center.* Rockville, MD: Westat, Inc.

Lehrer, Evelyn. 1983. "Determinants of Child Care Mode Choices: An Economic Perspective." *Social Science Research* 12(1): 69–80.

———. 1989. "Preschoolers with Working Mothers." *Journal of Population Economics* 1(4): 251–268.

Lehrer, Evelyn L., Teresa Santero, and Sumaria Mohan-Neill. 1991. "The Impact of Employer-Sponsored Child Care on Female Labor Supply Behavior: Evidence from the Nursing Profession." *Population Research and Policy Review* 10(3): 197–212.

Leibowitz, Arleen, Linda Waite, and Christina Witsberger. 1988. "Child Care for Preschoolers: Differences by Child's Age." *Demography* 25(2): 205–220.

Loomis, John, Armando Gonzalez-Caban, and Robin Gregory. 1994. "Do Reminders of Substitutes and Budget Constraints Influence Contingent Valuation Estimates?" *Land Economics* 70(4): 499–506.

Loomis, John B., Kerri Traynor, and Thomas Brown. 1999. "Trichotomous Choice: A Possible Solution to Dual Response Objectives in Dichotomous Choice Contingent Valuation Questions." *Journal of Agricultural and Resource Economics* 24(2): 572–583.

Marquart, Jules M. 1988. "A Pattern Matching Approach to Link Program Theory and Evaluation Data: The Case of Employer-Sponsored Child Care." Unpublished doctoral dissertation. Cornell University, Ithaca, NY.

Mason, Karen, and Karen Kuhlthau. 1989. "Determinants of Child Care Ideals among Mothers of Preschool-Aged Children." *Journal of Marriage and the Family* 51(3): 593–603.

Maume, David. 1991. "Child-care Expenditures and Women's Employment Turnover." *Social Forces* 70(2): 495–508.

McIntyre, Lee. 2000. "The Growth of Work-Site Daycare." *Regional Review: The Federal Reserve Bank of Boston* 10(3): 8–15.

Meyers, Marcia. 1997. "Cracks in the Seams: Durability of Child Care in JOBS Welfare-to-Work Programs." *Journal of Family and Economic Issues* 18(4): 379–406.

Milkovich, George T., and Lars R. Gomez. 1976. "Day Care and Selected Employee Work Behaviors." *Academy of Management Journal* 19(1): 111–115.

Miller, Thomas. 1984. "The Effects of Employer-Sponsored Child Care on Employee Absenteeism, Turnover, Productivity, Recruitment, and Job Satisfaction: What Is Claimed and What Is Known." *Personnel Psychology* 37(2): 277–289.

Mitchell, Anne, Louise Stoney, and Harriet Dichter. 2001. *Financing Child Care in the United States: An Expanded Catalog of Current Strategies.* Kansas City, MO: Ewing Marion Kauffman Foundation.

Mitchell, Robert Cameron, and Richard T. Carson. 1989. *Using Surveys to Value Public Goods: The Contingent Valuation Method.* Washington, DC: Resources for the Future.

Mocan, H. Naci. 2001. "Can Consumers Detect Lemons: Information Asymmetry in the Market for Child Care." NBER working paper no. 8291. Cambridge, MA: National Bureau of Economic Research.

Morrison, Mark D., Russell K. Blamey, and Jeff W. Bennett. 2000. "Minimising Payment Vehicle Bias in Contingent Valuation Studies." *Environmental and Resource Economics* 16(4): 407–422.

O'Connor, Martin, and Clive Spash, eds. 1999. *Valuation and the Environment: Theory, Method and Practice.* Northampton, MA: Elgar Publishing.

O'Connor, Richard M., Magnus Johannesson, and Per-Olov Johansson. 1999. "Stated Preferences, Real Behavior and Anchoring: Some Empirical Evidence." *Environmental and Resource Economics* 13(2): 235–248.

Olsen, Jan Abel. 1997. "Aiding Priority Setting in Health Care: Is There a Role for the Contingent Valuation Method?" *Health Economics* 6(6): 603–612.

Portney, Paul R. 1994. "The Contingent Valuation Debate: Why Economists Should Care." *Journal of Economic Perspectives* 8(4): 3–17.

Presser, Harriet. 1988. "Shift Work and Child Care among Young Dual-earner American Parents." *Journal of Marriage and the Family* 50(1): 133–148.

———. 1989. "Can We Make Time for Children? The Economy, Work Schedules, and Child Care." *Demography* 26(4): 523–543.

———. 1995. "Job, Family, and Gender: Determinants of Non-standard Work Schedules among Employed Americans in 1991." *Demography* 32(4): 577–598.

Ready, Richard C., Jean C. Buzby, and Dayman Hu. 1996. "Differences between Continuous and Discrete Contingent Valuation." *Land Economics* 72(3): 397–411.

Ribar, David. 1992. "Child Care and the Labor Supply of Married Women: Reduced Form Evidence." *Journal of Human Resources* 28(1):134–165.

———. 1995. "A Structural Model of Child Care and the Labor Supply of Married Women." *Journal of Labor Economics* 13(3): 558–597.

Ribaric, Ronald. 1987. "Mission Possible: Meeting Family Demands." *The Personnel Administrator* 32(8): 70–79.

Robins, Philip K. 1990. "Federal Financing of Child Care: Alternative Approaches and Economic Implications." *Population Research and Policy Review* 9(1): 65–90.

Roth, Maren, and Joanne Preston. 1989. "Career/Family Conflicts: The Subtle Drain on Corporate America." *Organization Development Journal* 7(2): 63–71.

Rothausen, Teresa, Jorge Gonzalez, Nicole Clarke, and Lisa O'Dell. 1998. "Family-Friendly Backlash—Fact or Fiction? The Case of Organizations' On-Site Child Care Centers." *Personnel Psychology* 51(3): 685–706.

Rubin, Victor, Phyllis Weinstock, Carol Chetkovich, and Laura Schlictmann. 1989. *Employer-Supported Child Care: Measuring and Understanding Its Impacts on the Workplace.* Berkeley, CA: Berkeley Planning Associates.

Samulari, Melissa, and Marilyn Manser. 1989. "Employer Provided Benefits: Employer Costs Versus Employee Value." *Monthly Labor Review* 112(12): 24–33.

Scarpa, Riccardo, and Ian Bateman. 2000. "Efficiency Gains Afforded by Improved Bid Design Versus Follow-up Valuation Questions in Discrete-Choice Contingent Valuation Studies." *Land Economics* 76(2): 299–311.

Sen, Amartya K. 1977. "Rational Fools: A Critique of the Behavioral Foundations of Economic Theory." *Philosophy and Public Affairs* 6(4): 317–344.

Seyler, Diane, Pamela Monroe, and James Garand. 1995. "Balancing Work and Family: The Role of Employer-Supported Child Care Benefits." *Journal of Family Issues* 16(2): 170–193.

Shellenbarger, Sue. 1992. "Work and Family: Work-Family Plans Cut Absenteeism, Stress." *Wall Street Journal*, January 20, p. B1.

Smith, Kristin. 2002. "Who Is Minding the Kids? Child Care Arrangements, Spring 1997." *Current Population Reports*, P70-86. Washington, DC: U.S. Census Bureau, Department of Commerce. http://www.census.gov/prod/2002pubs/p70-86.pdf.

Smith, V. Kerry. 1996. "Can Contingent Valuation Distinguish Economic Values for Different Public Goods?" *Land Economics* 72(2): 139–151.

Smith, V. Kerry and Laura Osborne. 1996. "Do Contingent Valuation Estimates Pass a 'Scope' Test? A Meta-Analysis." *Journal of Environmental Economics and Management* 31(3): 287–301.

Sonenstein, Freya. 1991. "The Child Care Preferences of Parents with Young Children: How Little Is Known." In *Parental Leave and Child Care: Setting a Research and Policy Agenda*, Janet Hyde and Marilyn Essex, eds. Philadelphia: Temple University Press, pp. 337–353.

Sonenstein, Freya, Gary Gates, Stefanie Schmidt, and Natalya Bolshun. 2002. "Primary Child Care Arrangements of Employed Parents: Findings from the 1999 National Survey of America's Families." Occasional paper no. 59. Washington, DC: Urban Institute.

Sprague, Peg. 1998. "Weighing Your Childcare Options." *HR Focus* 75(4): 13.

State of California. 1998. "Instructions for Form FTB 3501." California Tax Forms, p. 1.

State of Georgia. 1998. "Georgia Business Expansion and Support Act." Department of Revenue, Income Tax Division, p. 1.

Summers, Lawrence H. 1989. "Some Simple Economics of Mandated Benefits." *American Economic Review Papers and Proceedings* 79(2): 177–183.

Svedsater, Henrik. 2000. "Contingent Valuation of Global Environmental Resources: Tests of Perfect and Regular Embedding." *Journal of Economic Psychology* 21(6): 605–623.

Swallow, Stephen K., James J. Opaluch, and Thomas F. Weaver. 2001. "Strength-of-Preference Indicators and an Ordered-Response Model for

Ordinarily Dichotomous, Discrete Choice Data." *Journal of Environmental Economics and Management* 41(1): 70–93.

Taylor, Laura O., Michael McKee, Susan K. Laury, and Ronald G. Cummings. 2001. "Induced-value Tests of the Referendum Voting Mechanism." *Economics Letters* 71(1): 61–65.

U.S. Census Bureau. 1995. *Statistical Abstract of the United States*. http://www/census.gov/statab/www/ or http://www.census.gov/prod/www/statistical-abstract-us.html (accessed September 10, 2003).

———. 1998. PPL-81, Table A, Internet Release 1997. http://www.census.gov/population/www/socdemo/child/childcare98.html (accessed September 10, 2003).

———. 2000. *Statistical Abstract of the United States*. http://www/census.gov/statab/www/ or http://www.census.gov/prod/www/statistical-abstract-us.html (accessed September 10, 2003).

———. 2001. *Statistical Abstract of the United States*. http://www/census.gov/statab/www/ or http://www.census.gov/prod/www/statistical-abstract-us.html (accessed September 10, 2003).

———. 2002a. *Statistical Abstract of the United States*. http://www/census.gov/statab/www/ or http://www.census.gov/prod/www/statistical-abstract-us.html (accessed September 10, 2003).

———. 2002b. PPL-964, Table 2B, Internet Release 2002. http://www.census.gov/population/socdemo/child/ppl-964/tab02.pdf (accessed September 10, 2003).

———. 2003. PPL-168, Table 2B, Internet Release 2003. http://www.census.gov/population/socdemo/child/ppl-168/tab02B.txt (accessed: September 10, 2003).

U.S. Department of Labor. Bureau of Labor Statistics. 1999a. "Change in Percent of Persons Working Full-time Year Round Varies by Sex and Education." *Monthly Labor Review: The Editor's Desk*. September 24, 1999. http://www.bls.gov/opub/ted/1999/sept/wk4/art05.htm (accessed March 16, 2002).

———. 2002. Bureau of Labor Statistics. http://www.bls.gov/sahome.html (accessed March 19, 2002).

U.S. Department of the Treasury. 1998. "Investing in Child Care: Challenges Facing Working Parents and the Private Sector Response." Report 3110, April 15. Washington, DC: U.S. Department of the Treasury. http://www.treas.gov/press/releases/reports/chdcare.pdf (accessed September 10, 2003).

U.S. House of Representatives. 1997. *1997 Green Book: Overview of Entitlement Programs*. Washington, DC: U.S. Government Printing Office, p. 874.

Vandell, Deborah, and Barbara Wolfe. 2000. "Child Care Quality: Does It Matter and Does It Need to Be Improved?" Washington, DC: U.S. Department of Health and Human Services, Office of the Assistant Secretary for Planning and Evaluation, May. http://aspe.hhs.gov/search/hsp/ccquality00/report.pdf (accessed September 10, 2003).

Waite, Linda, Arleen Leibowitz, and Christina Witsberger. 1991. "What Parents Pay for: Child Care Characteristics, Quality, and Costs." *Journal of Social Issues* 47(2): 33–49.

Walker, James. 1991. "Public Policy and the Supply of Child Care Services." In *The Economics of Child Care*, David Blau, ed. New York: Russell Sage, pp. 51–77.

Wash, Patrick, and Liesel Brand. 1990. "Child Day Care Services: An Industry at a Crossroads." Monthly Labor Review 113(12): 17–24.

Whitehead, John C., Timothy C. Haab, and Ju-Chin Huang. 1998. "Part-Whole Bias in Contingent Valuation: Will Scope Effects Be Detected with Inexpensive Survey Methods?" *Southern Economic Journal* 65(1): 160–168.

Williams, Margaret, and Shelley MacDermid. 1994. "Linkages between Employee Benefits and Attitudinal and Behavioral Outcomes: A Research Review and Agenda." *Human Resource Management Review* 4(2): 131–160.

Witte, Ann D., and Magaly Queralt. 2002. "Take-Up Rates and Trade Offs after the Age of Entitlement: Some Thoughts and Empirical Evidence for Child Care Subsidies." NBER working paper no. 8886. Cambridge, MA: National Bureau of Economic Reseearch.

Woodbury, Stephen. 1990. "Economic Issues in Employee Benefits. In *Research in Labor Economics,* vol. 11, Laurie Bassi and David Crawford, eds. Greenwich, CT: JAI Press, pp. 271–296.

Youngblood, Stewart, and Kimberly Chambers-Cook. 1974. "Child Care Assistance Can Improve Employee Attitudes and Behavior." *Personnel Administrator* 19(2).

The Authors

Rachel Connelly is a professor of Economics at Bowdoin College and a nationally known scholar of the economics of child care. She has published articles on both the supply side and demand side of child care. Her early work on child care focused on the effect of child care costs on women's employment in the United States and on self-employed child care providers. In the late 1990s, Deborah S. DeGraff, Deborah Levison, and Connelly studied the relationship between child care and women's employment in Brazil. More recently she has studied child care mode choice (with Jean Kimmel and separately with Elizabeth Davis), child care workers (with Jean Kimmel) and this work on employer-sponsored child care (with Deborah S. DeGraff and Rachel A. Willis). Connelly also does research on human resource issues in China, particularly women's migration and rural education.

Deborah S. DeGraff is associate professor of Economics at Bowdoin College, where she has been a member of the faculty since 1991. Prior to that, she held an NICHD post-doctoral research fellowship at the Carolina Population Center of the University of North Carolina. Her research has focused primarily on demographic, labor force, and human resource issues in developing countries. She has published articles on the determinants of fertility and contraceptive use in the Philippines (with Richard E. Bilsborrow and David K. Guilkey) and in Bangladesh, and on the measurement of unmet need for family planning in Sri Lanka (with Victor de Silva). She has also analyzed children's schooling and work activities in the Philippines and Ecuador (with Richard E. Bilsborrow), young women's employment and unemployment in Sri Lanka (with Anju Malhotra), and child care and women's employment in Brazil, as indicated above. This work on employer-sponsored on-site child care is her first study based in the United States. In addition to grant support for this project from the W.E. Upjohn Institute for Employment Research, she has received support for her work from the Rockefeller Foundation, the Russell Sage Foundation, the National Science Foundation, the International Labour Office and USAID, as well as from Bowdoin College. DeGraff is a recipient of Bowdoin's Karofsky prize for teaching excellence, and she held the position of Associate Dean for Academic Affairs from 2000/01 through 2003/04.

Rachel A. Willis is associate professor of American Studies and Economics at University of North Carolina at Chapel Hill. Her research focuses on factors affecting access to work in the American economy with a special focus on manufacturing jobs in the southeastern United States Topics include work/family balance policies, transportation, education, gender, race, immigrant status, and health as they affect access to employment. She has received grants and fellowships from numerous sources including the Russell Sage and Rockefeller Foundations' Future of Work Program, the National Science Foundation, the Ford Foundation, the Department of Education, the Smith Richardson Foundation as well as the W.E. Upjohn Institute for Employment Research. Willis has won numerous teaching and public service awards for her research and public policy initiatives including the first Robert E. Bryan Public Service Award for her work on UNC's Public Service Center, on regional transit issues, and for policy contributions relating to North Carolina's Smart Start legislation which improved day care standards statewide.

Index

The italic letters *f*, *n*, and *t* following a page number indicate that the subject information of the heading is within a figure, note, or table, respectively, on that page.

About the Institute

The W.E. Upjohn Institute for Employment Research is a nonprofit research organization devoted to finding and promoting solutions to employment-related problems at the national, state, and local levels. It is an activity of the W.E. Upjohn Unemployment Trustee Corporation, which was established in 1932 to administer a fund set aside by the late Dr. W.E. Upjohn, founder of The Upjohn Company, to seek ways to counteract the loss of employment income during economic downturns.

The Institute is funded largely by income from the W.E. Upjohn Unemployment Trust, supplemented by outside grants, contracts, and sales of publications. Activities of the Institute comprise the following elements: 1) a research program conducted by a resident staff of professional social scientists; 2) a competitive grant program, which expands and complements the internal research program by providing financial support to researchers outside the Institute; 3) a publications program, which provides the major vehicle for disseminating the research of staff and grantees, as well as other selected works in the field; and 4) an Employment Management Services division, which manages most of the publicly funded employment and training programs in the local area.

The broad objectives of the Institute's research, grant, and publication programs are to 1) promote scholarship and experimentation on issues of public and private employment and unemployment policy, and 2) make knowledge and scholarship relevant and useful to policymakers in their pursuit of solutions to employment and unemployment problems.

Current areas of concentration for these programs include causes, consequences, and measures to alleviate unemployment; social insurance and income maintenance programs; compensation; workforce quality; work arrangements; family labor issues; labor-management relations; and regional economic development and local labor markets.

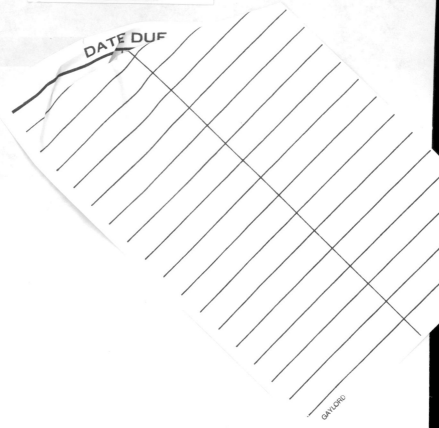

DATE DUE

GAYLORD

PRINTED IN U